plants
for free

plants for free

how to create a garden for next-to-nothing

Sharon Amos

Photography by Steve Wooster

C&B

COLLINS & BROWN

With grateful thanks to Anne Tester, Doreen Amos and
Nick Tester for sharing their gardening wisdom.

First published in Great Britain in 2001 by
Collins & Brown Limited
London House
Great Eastern Wharf
Parkgate Road
London SW11 4NQ

1 3 5 7 9 8 6 4 2

British Library Cataloguing-in-Publication Data:
A catalogue record for this book is available from the British Library.

ISBN 1 85585 872 X

Senior Editor: Clare Churly
Editor: Alison Leach
Horticultural consultant: Tony Lord
Design: Liz Brown
Photography: Steve Wooster and George Taylor
Illustrator: Ian Sidaway

Reproduction by Global Colour, Malaysia
Printed and bound in Hong Kong by C&C Offset Printing Company

This book was typeset using Fairfield and GillSans.

The publishers would like to thank the following nurseries and gardens for providing plants for photography: The
Beth Chatto Gardens, Forest Lodge Garden Centre, Farnham and Wyevale Garden Centre, Enfield.

Collins & Brown/Jacqui Hurst 138, 138–9, /**David Markson** 126–7, /**Howard Rice** 20(t), 40–1, 48–9(t),
50–1, 60–1, 61, 62–3, 64–5, 74–5, 76–7, 80–1, 81, 82–3, 87, 89, 92–3(t), 98–9, 102–3, 112–13, 118–19(t), 130–1,
140–1; **Jerry Harpur** 133; **Marcus Harpur** 48–9(b), 116, 128; **George Taylor** 14–19, 21–6, 28–9;
Steve Wooster 1, 2, 6 (Hadspen House), 7(t & b) (Beth Chatto Gardens), 8–9 (Butterstream), 10, 11(l). 11(r), 12
(Beth Chatto Gardens), 13, 27 (Briar Rose Cottage), 30–1 (Yalding Organic Gardens), 32 (Beth Chatto Gardens),
33 (Broughton Castle), 35 (Ram House), 36 (Beth Chatto Gardens), 37 (Beth Chatto Gardens), 38, 39 (Beth
Chatto Gardens), 42–3, 44, 44–5 (Beth Chatto Gardens), 46–7, 47, 50, 52, 52–3, 54, 54–5, 56–7, 58, 58–9 (Beth
Chatto Gardens), 64, 66, 66–7, 68–9, 69, 70–1, 71, 72 (Briar Rose Cottage), 72–3, 75, 77, 78–9, 79, 83, 84–5, 85,
86–7 (Beth Chatto Gardens), 88–9, 90, 90–1, 92–3(b), 94, 94–5, 96–7 (Beth Chatto Gardens), 97, 100–1, 101,
103, 104–5, 106, 106–7, 108, 108–9 (Beth Chatto Gardens), 110, 110–11, 113, 114–15, 115, 116–7, 118–9(b)
(Beth Chatto Gardens), 120–1 (Beth Chatto Gardens), 121, 122–3, 123, 124–5, 125, 127, 128–9, 131, 132–3, 134,
134–5, 136, 136–7, 141.

contents

Introduction

Filling your garden with plants needn't cost a fortune. There are plenty of species that multiply and make more plants without any help from you at all – or with the very minimum of assistance. And very often these are plants that friends, neighbours and family will have in their gardens and be delighted to share.

This approach to gardening is the complete opposite to coming home from the garden centre with a boot full of plants and no clear idea where to put them or how to grow them. By sharing cuttings and small plants with other gardeners, you'll also be acquiring vital information. You'll have seen the mature plants growing in their gardens. You'll know how tall they grow and how wide they spread. You can see what other plants they look good with and you'll have learned what growing conditions they need. Every plant you receive in this way will come with some advice, however pithy. And when you are ready to pass on plants, you'll find that you too will be ready with advice

on where they are likely to thrive. It's not a new way of gardening – it's been going on since time immemorial.

Bartering and recycling are ingrained in human nature, and for gardeners on a budget there are no better ways to make a garden. Throwing money indiscriminately at a garden can't guarantee your borders will be filled with beautiful flowers and stunning shrubs. But by following a few simple guidelines, you can create a garden bursting with fabulous flowers and foliage. And, with plants to spare, you can swap with friends, or use them to stock a plant stall at a fund-raising event or local summer fair.

You don't need any special equipment – most of what you are likely to need can be improvised or recycled from things already lying around in the garden or garage. Nor do you need any particular expertise – where any techniques are needed, they are the very simplest of all.

Every plant listed in the directory is there for very specific reasons. It is easy to grow, makes good-sized plants in a short space of time, or covers the ground quickly; it either self-seeds or it can be propagated very simply – and so

Prolific self-seeders *Although poppy flowers rarely last more than a few days, they are produced in profusion and form great drifts of colour.*

produce plants for free. Just because a plant is easy to grow and propagate doesn't mean it is commonplace – many unusual or less well-known species have these qualities, too.
The directory does not claim to be exhaustive, but it does aim to suggest some good starter plants. You'll probably soon have some ideas of your own to add to it.

Of course, when you are creating a garden on a new plot, the trade is going to be rather one way and you will initially be relying on the generosity of family, friends and neighbours to give you plants or cuttings. You may also have to spend a little money on buying plants from local markets, plant fairs and fund-raising events. But that is how you'll track down some of the more unusual species and build up stocks to repay the people who got you started in the first place – and to barter for new plants they've since acquired.

Instant height
Aaron's rod, or mullein, is a biennial, forming a rosette of furry leaves in its first year, before sending up 6ft (1.8m) flowering stems the following summer.

Spring colour
Once you've sown forget-me-nots in your garden, you'll never be without them, as they self-seed year after year. Here they surround columbine, another spring-flowering self-seeding species.

GETTING STARTED

Finding plants

All of the plants described in this book are prolific self-seeders that produce lots more plants every year, are easily propagated from simple cuttings, or spread rapidly so that they can be divided up to make more plants – and you can fill up your garden with plants at little expense. If, however, you are starting a garden from scratch, it would be short-sighted to depend solely on contributions from other gardeners to fill your flower beds. You will have to make a small initial outlay to buy some plants that you can propagate and begin sharing with family, friends and neighbours.

For plants of the highest quality at prices that won't dent your budget, there are a number of other options available to simply calling in at the nearest commercial garden centre.

Fairs, garden gate and boot sales

These are probably the cheapest source of plants. Look on the bulletin board in your supermarket, or in the local newspaper, for details of sales and fairs in the section advertising forthcoming events. Car boot sales can yield bargains, but be wary of plants being sold off cheaply as they may be past their prime. Many fairs have a plant stall and it's worth arriving early for the best selection.

If seeds have a good germination rate, gardeners can end up with far too many plants.

… get started by stocking up with home-grown plants at summer fairs …

… violas and pansies germinate readily, leaving gardeners with plants to spare …

Look out for signs on garden gates offering surplus plants very cheaply – very often they will be set out on a table at the gate, with an honesty box for you to make your payment. Pansies (*Viola* x *wittrockiana*), marigolds (*Tagetes*), stocks (*Matthiola incana*) and many annuals are likely to be surplus to requirements. Tender plants, like pelargoniums and petunias may also be available from these sources.

Farmers' markets

Farmers' markets are a growing phenomenon. They began in the United States over a hundred years ago, declined with the advent of supermarkets, but are enjoying a huge revival in both the US and UK as a way of bringing fresh fruit, vegetables and plants into cities and towns. It is not, of course, only in major cities that farmers' markets flourish – they are also held in numerous other towns across the country. Such markets are increasingly recognised as being not only a great place to buy plants and fresh produce, but also a means of supporting small,

… farmers' markets are a good source of top-quality plants …

independent growers. All farmers and growers setting up stalls must be from within a fixed local radius and must be selling home-grown produce. Plants sold by independent growers at farmers' markets are often of superior quality: selling directly to their customers week after week is a strong incentive to build up a good reputation.

If possible, go regularly to a farmers' market so you can get to know the growers. That way, you can make special requests for plants that you are looking for and receive plenty of tips about growing them. Even if the nearest market is some distance away, it is often well worth making a special expedition. Check the local paper to find out when and where they're held.

Open garden schemes

Summer open days for groups of private village or city gardens are becoming increasingly popular and at least one garden on the circuit is bound to be selling plants at a reasonable price.

There are also a number of national organisations that run open garden schemes, such as the National Gardens Scheme (NGS) in the UK and Australia's Open Gardens Scheme. Such schemes raise money for charity by charging a modest admission fee to a carefully

---

CHOOSING PLANTS

Plants sold by producers at farmers' markets have standards to maintain, so they will invariably be good quality. If buying at car boot sales or fund-raising events remember the following tips:
• Look for plants that are well established. Avoid droopy specimens, which may simply have been dug up and potted that day, without time to root properly. A few roots emerging from the pot's drainage holes indicates a healthy root system.
• Choose plants with plenty of buds and fresh new growth.
• Avoid plants with any withered, scorched or distorted leaves.
• Avoid plants that have any weeds growing in the pot.

inspected. selection of private gardens. The income from plant stalls will go to a good cause, so it's money well spent.

Remember that by visiting other people's gardens you often get a valuable lesson in planting and cultivation, as well as a chance of buying some of the very plants you've admired, knowing they've been grown with loving care by an enthusiast.

More fund-raising sales

Other charitable organisations hold regular fund-raising sales and their plant stalls can be an unrivalled source of good plants at rock-bottom prices. Look out for weekly markets advertised in your local press. all over the country. The National Trust also holds plant sales at their properties and, while this won't be one the cheapest ways to buy plants, you will be able to

meet growers from specialist nurseries and acquire some unusual and top-quality plants to increase your stocks.

Many villages and local communities operate informal open days, or 'garden safaris', very often with plant stalls to raise funds for specific projects, such as church repairs, or to contribute to a new village hall. Once you get started, you might even consider organising your own!

Arboreta and botanical gardens

If you are keen to learn more about plants, try visiting your nearest arboretum or botanical garden. Depending on the location, they vary considerably in size, and in the types of plants grown. Many of these places have education departments that offer guided tours and regular classes for the general public. Where classes are

… you will often find more unusual species for sale on tours of private gardens …

... look for healthy plants with plenty of fresh, new growth ...

available, they will provide you with easy access to a wealth of expert knowledge and experience that will be especially pertinent to your local growing conditions.

The Internet

If you have access to the Internet, you can use your browser to find Web pages devoted to every aspect of gardening. You can make contact with other enthusiasts and share tips. You can check if a particular plant will flourish in your area. The main drawback of the Internet is that it holds such a vast store of information that you could find yourself spending more time browsing than actually working in your garden!

IF YOU DO BUY BADLY

If you do accidentally end up buying a plant that is pot-bound, don't despair. You may be able to rescue it. Tap the pot to loosen the root ball and gently pull the plant out. If its roots are growing out through the drainage holes in the bottom of the pot, you may have to cut the pot away. Try to disentangle some of the roots so that they are not spiralling around and around or – in really severe cases – cut away some of them. Then plant it out in a prepared hole: loosen the soil at the bottom of the hole with a fork, to help enfeebled roots grow down. Try to splay some of the plant's roots out before you firm back the soil, then water in thoroughly.

Improvising tools and equipment

The key to improvisation in the garden is to see a potential value in everything and to throw away as little as possible. If you can't immediately think of a use for some old cupboard doors, or some windows you've had replaced, tuck them away in a corner until you need them. You could use them to make a cold frame (see page 16), or lash the doors together around four wooden posts to make a compost container. Keep squares of old carpet to cover compost containers, or to smother weeds when clearing a patch of ground.

Think how thrifty our ancestors were. Old iron bed frames, for example, stood on end in the vegetable plot as a trellis to support runner beans, or even to block a gap in a hedge until the shrubs grew big enough – they certainly wouldn't have ended up at the tip.

The basics

You really don't need a shed full of equipment to maintain the average small garden and while you may have to invest in one or two essential tools, many others just call for a bit of lateral thinking.

You are always going to need a spade, a fork and a trowel, and these can often be picked up cheaply at car boot sales, or in second-hand shops, especially those that handle house clearances. A dibber for making holes in the soil for small plants and bulbs is no better than a bit of old broom handle, while two small wooden sticks and a length of twine have been used for centuries to mark out straight lines or curves.

Essential tools *The biggest investment you may need to make is in a spade and a fork – try to buy second-hand if your budget is tight. Bamboo canes are inexpensive and you'll soon build up a stock of spare plastic pots through swapping plants.*

Free cloches *Cut-down plastic bottles make useful mini-cloches to protect small plants and are surprisingly durable*

Cloches and cat-scarers

Clear plastic pop or mineral water bottles are often labelled recyclable, yet it may be difficult to find a local centre that has facilities for recycling plastic. So to ease your conscience as well as save money in the garden, cut them down to make mini-cloches for protecting individual plants from the worst of the weather or from pest attack. The top sections with the narrow neck, or the dimpled bases, make good cloches, while open-ended, central sections can be useful for protecting small plants from being uprooted by cats or birds.

If cats are a problem in your garden, scratching up newly sown seed or small plants and leaving behind their undesirable calling cards, many gardeners swear by this modern cat-scarer. Half-fill an empty clear plastic bottle with water and lay it on its side in the area you want to keep cat-free. Cats appear to dislike the changing reflections it makes.

Pots and potting mixtures

The vast number of small plastic plant pots in circulation in the gardening world means that

you are very unlikely ever to need to buy any. They are like a sort of currency that just keeps changing hands – practically every plant that you acquire will be in a pot, which can be washed and reused numerous times. If you are just getting started and truly feel that you are running short, ask a neighbour. Most people have dozens of spare plastic pots that they will be only too pleased to pass on to someone who wants them.

Making your own potting mixture is time-consuming and tricky, and this is one instance when a trip to the garden centre for the biggest sack you can buy is money well spent.

Improvised cat-scarer *Cats really do appear to be discouraged from making free in the flower beds where simple water-bottle cat-scarers are in place. Once plants are growing strongly and covering bare earth, the scarers can be removed.*

Instant cold frame *A cheap plastic storage crate – the sort commonly sold to tidy up toys – makes an instant cold frame with a sheet of perspex for a lid. Set the lid at an angle to allow ventilation on warm days.*

Making a cold frame

The principle behind a conventional cold frame is to insulate small pots of cuttings against the worst of winter weather. But you don't need an expensive custom-built model. Something as unsophisticated as a wooden or plastic crate with a sheet of perspex or glass across the top can be a cold frame – if it works, who cares what it looks like? A small crate can be fitted into a corner very easily in even the tiniest garden. For more ambitious gardeners, a homemade construction of a couple of old doors nailed to posts with some old windows for lids and boards to form the sides will hold a lot more plants until they're ready to go out into their final positions in the garden.

Inexpensive cane caps
Prevent accidents by capping canes with empty vitamin C tubes. If you have time, paint them green to help them blend in amongst foliage.

Canes, cane caps and plant supports

Some tall plants manage perfectly well without stakes, but there are many species that do need a helping hand, especially in windy weather, or on exposed sites. Bamboo canes are the classic answer. If you have space, you could grow a small patch of bamboo, such as *Pseudosasa amabilis*, specifically to harvest your own canes, as this is an ideal way of keeping vigorous bamboo species under control. Keep a look out in your area, especially where gardens are large – you may come across handwritten notices advertising homegrown bamboo canes for sale at a modest price. Reasonably long straight prunings from your own garden shrubs and trees can also make useful stakes.

To avoid nasty accidents, every cane needs a cap. Empty tubes of fizzy vitamin C tablets – or, dare it be said, denture cleaning tablets – are ideal as they are deep enough and narrow enough to stay on the cane without blowing away. Admittedly, they don't look that attractive, but once a plant grows taller, the foliage may disguise the cane cap. Or you could paint them with any spare green gloss paint that you happen to have lying around. Painting canes can help them blend in better too, as although newly cut bamboo is green, it dries to more noticeable yellow brown.

In a community wood or forest, you may be able to get permission to cut small amounts of hazel, ash or willow coppicing, which you can use to make your own plant supports – wigwams for sweet peas (*Lathyrus odoratus*), roughly woven trellis for other climbers. Try to use the thinnest twigs to weave in and out to form the horizontal bands on a wigwam; if they are not pliable enough, soak them in the bath for a couple of hours. If you still have difficulty weaving with them, try using raffia, split cane or wire instead – anything you have to hand in the shed.

When bamboo is fresh, it is flexible enough to be bent into domed supports for lower growing plants that nevertheless can be flattened and spoiled by heavy rain plus wind – for example, some of the larger hardy geraniums, peonies (*Paeonia*) and poppies (*Papaver*). Simply push one end of the bamboo into the ground close to the plant and form it into a hoop, pushing the other end into the soil too. Repeat to build up an inverted basket shape. You can also use willow for this technique, though you run the risk of the plant support itself taking root. One way to avoid this is to strip the bark off. In rural gardens, wild willow species often form part of informal hedges and boundaries and most gardeners will be happy to supply you with some stems.

Making a compost container

An old galvanised dustbin with the bottom knocked out makes a discreet compost container in a small garden. Add uncooked kitchen scraps – fruit and vegetable peelings, tea bags, coffee grounds, crushed eggshells – grass cuttings, weeds and spent plants (provided they are not diseased). Add some cardboard and scrunched up newspaper to aerate the pile and stop the compost getting too sloppy. If you keep rabbits or guinea pigs, add their hay or straw bedding plus droppings when you clean their cages. Compost can be ready to use to enrich soil in the flower borders in around six months. In a bigger garden, try making a compost container from old wooden pallets lashed together, with a square of old carpet for a lid.

Building a simple wigwam *A simple, rustic wigwam of thin stems of coppiced ash adds height and interest to a border even before it is swathed in climbing plants. Use it to support nasturtiums or sweet peas.*

Saving and sowing seed

Plants that self-seed are a joy. They take away all the hard work of preparing a seedbed or messing around with seed trays on a spare bedroom windowsill. The seed germinates naturally at the right time and very often earlier in the year than a gardener would risk, giving plants a head start. There's something very satisfying about knowing that you can rely on species like pot marigolds (*Calendula officinalis*), love-in-a-mist (*Nigella damascena*), forget-me-nots (*Myosotis sylvatica*) and foxgloves (*Digitalis purpurea*) to produce a whole new generation of plants year after year.

To take advantage of a plant's capacity to self-seed, you must not be too tidy. You need to leave seedheads on a plant to give the seed time to disperse. This can have all sorts of other benefits too. One is improving the garden habitat for seed-eating birds: you can afford to be generous and share seed of prolific plants like hollyhocks (*Alcea rosea*) and evening primroses (*Oenothera biennis*) with small birds such as goldfinches and sparrows. Many seedheads, particularly those of umbellifers, look beautiful in winter with a tracery of hoar frost outlining their intricate structure. Dead stems can also offer a small but significant amount of extra frost-protection to dormant plants in winter.

Until you become adept at recognising the leaves of seedlings, it is not a good idea to fork up the surface of the soil around existing plants,

or to use a hoe to weed indiscriminately in the borders — you may be hoeing away some interesting plants as you do so.

Transplanting

Some self-seeding species are tricky to transplant. Love-in-a-mist, clarkia (*Clarkia unguiculata*, syn. *C. elegans*) and California poppies (*Eschscholzia californica*) don't usually survive being moved to a new position in the garden, but there are several things you can do to make sure you get at least some plants in the right place. One is to shake ripe seedheads (or even the whole plant if it is an annual and has finished flowering) over the patch of ground where you'd like more plants. Or you can save seed to sow yourself in the open ground the following spring (see below).

Saving seed

For best results, leave seedheads to ripen on the plant for as long as possible and then cut them off just before the seed is released. This can be a difficult point to judge and it may be easier to cut down the whole plant stem when it is quite dry. Tie paper bags over the individual seedheads and hang the stem upside down in a dry, airy room to complete the process. Always use paper bags to catch seed rather than plastic: paper lets the plant material dry out still further, whereas

HOW TO STORE SEED

1 With a single seedhead you can tap seed directly onto a small piece of sharply creased paper. A single poppy head yields hundreds of seeds; a whole plant will keep family, friends and neighbours supplied too.

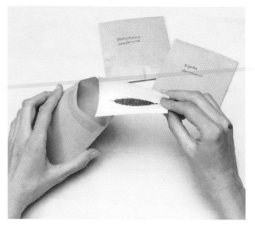

2 Use the crease to channel the seed into a labelled envelope. Always remember to label your saved seed. For best results and highest germination rates, don't store seed for longer than a year or two.

plastic bags retain moisture and may make seedheads rot.

Foxgloves can be rather difficult to handle, but they produce seed by the sackful so it doesn't matter if you lose a lot on the way – just shake spent stems over a sheet of white paper and you'll have more than enough seed for you and your neighbours.

Once the seedheads have opened, transfer the seed into labelled paper envelopes to store. A sharp crease in a piece of paper makes an easy way to channel seed into an envelope. Place the envelopes in an airtight, mouse-proof container and store them in a cool, frost-free place until ready to sow next year. Some seeds may need teasing out of their pods or capsules; hollyhock seeds, for example, can be quite tightly packed.

Sowing seed

Sowing seed in the open ground is the fastest way to get results, though be prepared for casualties along the way to slugs, snails and other pests, as well as birds. Make sure your patch of ground is free of weeds and stones, then rake the soil to break it down until it is fine and crumbly. Water the soil before you start – if you do it after, you risk washing the seed away. Then mark shallow, parallel furrows or 'drills' with a stick and sow the seed in these lines. This will be a guide when they start to germinate, as the seedlings should be identifiable because they're growing in lines, whereas weeds will not be.

Don't worry that the final planting will look regimented – once the plants grow bigger, it will be impossible to detect that the seed was sown in straight lines. If you are still afraid that you won't be able to tell plant seedlings from weeds, sow a few plant seeds in a pot of potting mixture (which will have been sterilised to destroy any weed seeds) and, when they have grown their second pair of 'true' leaves, use these as an identification guide to help you weed out any pretenders in the flower bed.

The classic time to sow seed is in spring, when the soil has warmed up a little after winter, but you can also get a head start by sowing seed of some species in the early autumn, before the soil starts to cool down. By doing a mixture of both, you can achieve the longest flowering season possible, by extending it at either end.

HOW TO SOW SEED

1 Water your seed bed, then create seed 'drills' (shallow furrows) by drawing a stick firmly through the soil (½in/1.5cm is the average depth). Make the distance between the drills at least 6in (15cm) apart.

2 Tip some seed into the palm of your hand and scatter it thinly along the seed drill. If you do sow too thickly, seedlings of many species can be thinned out.

3 Push the soil back gently over the seed. It's a good idea to mark rows with a stick, tagged with a piece of coloured wool perhaps, and note down species in a garden log book, or on a garden plan.

Cuttings

Bewildering references to different sorts of cuttings – softwood, semi-ripe, and hardwood – can sound complicated, but it helps if you remember that these terms really refer to cuttings taken at different times of year: softwood in spring, when growth is new and 'soft'; semi-ripe in summer, when growth is starting to firm up and mature, but the tips are still soft; and hardwood in the autumn, when stems are positively woody. Herbaceous perennials and fuchsias are usually propagated by softwood cuttings; many shrubs root easily from semi-ripe cuttings; while hardwood cuttings are suitable for many deciduous trees and shrubs. (See also root cuttings, page 25).

Increasing your plant stock *Fuchsias root easily from softwood cuttings and quickly make good growth. Really thrifty gardeners will even root the small growing tips that they've pinched out to promote bushy growth in new plants.*

Softwood Cutting
A cutting of the current season's growth taken when plant tissue is soft and pliable.

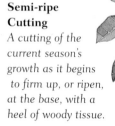

Semi-ripe Cutting
A cutting of the current season's growth as it begins to firm up, or ripen, at the base, with a heel of woody tissue.

Softwood cuttings

When choosing stems for softwood cuttings, avoid any with flower buds, as these will take far longer to root. Use a sharp knife to sever the stem close to where it joins the plant and carefully trim off the lower leaves. Use a pencil to make several holes in a pot of compost and insert several cuttings in one pot – as well as being economical, this also seems to have a beneficial influence on rooting. You can dip them in hormone rooting compound first, if you want to, but using too much can damage the stem.

Firm the cuttings in gently, water them and cover the pot with a plastic bag to make a mini-cloche. Don't let the leaves touch the plastic.

TAKING CUTTINGS

For best results, take cuttings from healthy, well-established plants. Choose vigorous shoots and avoid stems with diseased or damaged leaves. Don't choose stems with flower buds as they'll take much longer to root. As a general rule, the newer and fresher the growth, the quicker the cutting will root. Unfortunately, these shoots are also the most prone to wilting, so act quickly to get them into ideal growing conditions and keep the cuttings in a sealed plastic bag until you are ready to work. Use a proprietory growing medium, which will have been sterilized.

Check the cuttings regularly, and once roots have begun to show through the holes in the bottom of the pot, remove the plastic bag and pot them on into individual pots. This could take a couple of months. (See also transplanting, page 26).

You can also root softwood cuttings in water. Fill a jam jar with water and put a small piece of wire or plastic netting across the neck of the jar to hold the cuttings in place. With this method you can see at a glance when cuttings have rooted.

Semi-ripe cuttings

Cuttings that are semi-ripe tend to root more readily if taken with a 'heel' – a sliver of the main stem pulled away with the cutting. The cutting should be at least 3–4in (7.5–10cm) long. If taking cuttings from a friend's or neighbour's garden, immediately put them in a plastic bag and tie the top, to keep them until you can plant them – preferably later that day. When ready to plant, trim off the lower leaves and, if the remaining leaves are large, cut them in half to help reduce wilting. Then follow exactly the same procedure for potting up softwood cuttings (see left).

Rooting cuttings in a jar *Keep a handful of sweet woodruff cuttings in a jam jar on the kitchen windowsill and you'll find they've rooted within a couple of weeks. A net cover holds stems in place.*

1 Once you've taken cuttings, put them in a plastic bag and seal the top. Keep them there until you are ready to pot them up. Try to do this as soon as possible.

2 Moisten some potting mixture, squeeze off any excess water and fill a small pot. Use a pencil to make three or four holes in the mixture and insert a cutting in each, stripping off the lower leaves first.

3 Cover the pot with a plastic bag to act as a mini-cloche to conserve moisture and warmth. Use an elastic band to hold it firmly round the rim of the pot.

Hardwood cuttings

Take hardwood cuttings of deciduous trees and shrubs, including roses, once they have lost their leaves in autumn or early winter. These cuttings need minimum attention and can go straight in the garden, but it's a good idea to make a 'nursery trench' to keep them all in one place. This needn't take up lots of space or look ugly: you can hide it away at the back of a border, for example. Dig the trench about 4in (10cm) deep and put a layer of sharp sand or gravel in the bottom. Then prepare the cuttings. Take cuttings slightly longer than you need, so that you can trim off any soft tips to just above a bud. Trim the base to just below a bud, so that you are left with a stem 5–6in (13–15cm) long. Space the cuttings evenly in the trench and firm them in. Keep the area well weeded. Check after frost and re-firm cuttings if necessary. Most will be ready to transplant in a year's time.

HOW TO PLANT YOUR HARDWOOD CUTTINGS

1 Push a spade into the soil to about two-thirds of its depth and rock it backwards and forwards a short way to make a narrow V-shaped trench. Sprinkle some horticultural sand in the bottom for good drainage.

2 Space cuttings evenly – at least 4in (10cm) apart. Two-thirds of their stems should be below ground. Firm the soil back round them. Check after winter frosts and firm the cuttings back in again if the soil has lifted.

TAKING HARDWOOD CUTTINGS

•Take hardwood cuttings in the mid to late autumn for the best results.

•If possible, choose a sheltered spot for a nursery trench. If the soil is heavy, dig in some grit or well-rotted manure to improve drainage a few weeks before you plant the cuttings.

•Many roses are surprisingly easy to propagate by hardwood cuttings. Choose stems that have already flowered to improve chances of success still further. They should be the thickness of a pencil and about 6in (15cm) long and the thorns should be removed before planting.

Hardwood Cutting
A cutting of the current season's growth made up of woody, fully mature tissue, taken after the leaves have fallen naturally.

Layering

Layering occurs naturally in many plants when a stem that touches the ground puts down roots and eventually forms a new plant. To take advantage of this useful habit, you can always hurry nature along a little and encourage stems to layer using the following technique.

Shrubs such as winter jasmine (*Jasminum nudiflorum*) and climbers like akebia (*Akebia quinata*) increase naturally by layering. To encourage them, choose a long flexible stem and bend it down to soil level. Take off any leaves where the stem touches the soil, then hold it firmly in place with a wire peg – an old-fashioned hairpin is ideal, though it may not be strong enough if the stem is very whippy. In this case, a tent peg may be better. Scrape up some soil around the stem to cover it. (You can try making a tiny, shallow cut on the underside of the stem where it touches the ground, as the 'wound' helps to speed up root formation).

Leave the layered stem for anything from a couple of months to a year, then check that it has rooted by gently brushing away some soil where the stem touches the ground. If it has rooted, cut through the stem attaching it to the main plant, dig it up, and replant in its new position. To make replanting easier, you could peg the original stem into a small pot of potting mixture sunk level with the soil.

To get the maximum number of plantlets from a stem, you can layer it at several different points, as long as you leave a pair of leaves or leaf nodes between each layering point. Layering is best done in the autumn, but if you spot a naturally occurring layered stem that has already rooted, dig it up and replant it at any time except when the ground is frozen.

LAYERING TIP

Improve the soil where you are going to layer a plant by digging in some garden compost or well-rotted manure. If the soil is heavy, try adding some grit or gravel – tender young roots will rot in wet soil. If you are worried that the free end of a layered shoot may catch the breeze and disturb the layered section and its new roots, use a vertical stake to hold the free end in place.

LAYERING SHRUBS AND CLIMBERS

1 Choose a long flexible stem and bend it down to soil level. Nicking the stem on the underside with a sharp knife, to wound it, can speed up the formation of roots.

2 Pin the stem down firmly with a 'hairpin' of wire. A springy stem may need a stronger peg, or you can even try carefully weighting it down with a stone.

3 Cover the layered section with soil and water it well. Water regularly and keep an eye on it – within six months it should have rooted. You can check by gently brushing away some soil.

Dividing

Dividing is a really logical way of making more plants from a clump that has outgrown its position in the border and become over-dominant. It also has positive benefits for perennial plants, as they will almost certainly grow with renewed vigour and produce more and better flowers after dividing.

Division is traditionally done in autumn, when plants are approaching their dormant phase, but many species can be divided in spring, when it is easier to spot new strong buds appearing, and split them up without damaging them.

Start by digging the entire plant out of the border – using a fork avoids slicing through too many roots. Lay the plant on a sheet of newspaper so that you can see what you're doing. Small clumps can be divided fairly easily just by pulling them apart with your hands, or by using a trowel, but big clumps with an impossible tangle of roots may need a bit of force. Borrow a

DIVIDING

1 Start by digging up the whole clump – using a fork reduces the chance of damaging roots – and laying it on a sheet of newspaper.

2 Divide into smaller pieces using your hands or a trowel. Some species split easily into plantlets, but others have a dense central crown that may need to be divided with a knife. Discard any tired or tatty pieces and replant or pot up the rest immediately.

DIVIDING BEARDED IRISES

1 Dig up a clump of overcrowded irises after they have flowered. Separate the clump into portions of rhizome with leaves attached.

2 Choose firm, young pieces. Cut these into smaller portions using a sharp knife, making sure each has roots and leaves attached.

3 Trim the leaves to stop the wind lifting the plantlets before their roots have established. Replant with most of the rhizome above ground.

neighbour's garden fork and push it in at an angle into the centre of the clump, back-to-back with your own fork. Bring the two handles together to lever the plant roots apart at the same time.

Choose pieces of plant from the outside of the clump, as these will be the youngest and most strongly growing. You can safely throw away the central portion of an old clump of Michaelmas daisies (*Aster novi-belgii*) or phlox without fear of wastage as it's done its job. Replant the pieces directly into their new flowering position, watering them in well and continuing to water them regularly until they become established. If replanting some pieces in the original spot, dig in some well-rotted manure to revitalise the soil first.

For plants that need a modified version of this technique – bugle, for example – see the details under the relevant entry in the plant directory.

Root cuttings are an alternative to division and can yield a lot more plants if successfully carried out. They are suitable for plants with fat,

fleshy roots – Oriental poppies (*Papaver orientale*), for example, and bleeding hearts (*Dicentra formosa*). Dig up a plant in the autumn, or on a mild winter day, and brush off some soil so you can see the roots. Cut off a large root and replant the original plant. You need to remember which way up the root was growing. One way to do this is to cut the end of the root closest to the soil surface straight across, and mark the base with an oblique cut. Section the root into smaller pieces, between 2–3in (5–7.5cm) long, using the same cutting technique for easy identification. Place all the pieces the right way up in a pot of potting mixture, with the tops level with the surface of the mixture. Cover with a sprinkling of sand and leave in a cold frame, if possible, or a very sheltered spot, preferably with a plastic cloche over the pot.

By summer, cuttings that have rooted will have developed leaves and can be potted on before planting out permanently in the garden in the autumn.

ROOT CUTTINGS

1 Use a sharp knife to cut off just one thick root from a plant, about the thickness of a pencil, then return the parent plant to the border.

2 Cut the root into smaller pieces around 2–3in (5–7.5cm) long. Mark the top of each root with a straight cut and make an oblique cut across each base.

3 Insert four or five cuttings right way up in a pot of potting mixture, keeping the tops level with the surface.

4 Cover with a thin layer of horticultural sand and place the pot in a cold frame, or cover with a mini-cloche. Cuttings should have rooted and sprouted by summer.

Transplanting

Plants produced by division can generally be put straight in the ground in their new flowering positions, with the only proviso that they may need extra watering during hot spells and, if they are particularly small, an eye kept on them to make sure they are not swamped by neighbouring species or weeds. If the newly divided plants were in full leaf, it can be a good idea to trim away some of the foliage so that it doesn't make heavy demands on the root system, which is not yet fully developed.

Growing on cuttings

Plants produced from cuttings tend to need slightly more care. They tend to get lost in the general medley of the borders – bare hardwood cuttings thrust into gaps at random might be mistaken for simple markers and be pulled out by mistake (see page 21 for details on digging a nursery trench). Small softwood cuttings are vulnerable to wilting and need a more protected environment. The very best place to keep them is in labelled pots in a cold frame, that can be kept more or less open, but shaded, throughout the summer, then covered in autumn and winter to provide a small but vital amount of protection from freezing temperatures and searing winds.

If you have no space for a cold frame (see page 14) improvise during the summer by potting up cuttings and putting a clear plastic bag over the stems and pot. Take care that the bag doesn't touch the leaves and keep it in place with an elastic band around the pot. This creates a mini-cloche that is very effective in controlling moisture and temperature levels. Try to stand pots of cuttings on a north-facing windowsill in a room where you'll see them every day and can keep a close eye on their progress.

Whether in a cold frame or on a windowsill, once cuttings have rooted and are growing strongly, separate them and pot them up individually. Either keep them in a cool spare bedroom over winter – you can dispense with the plastic bag – or return to the cold frame. Or you could put them into a sheltered corner of the garden and insulate the pots by wrapping them with bubblewrap and adding a layer of straw all

TRANSPLANTING CUTTINGS

1 Check pots of cuttings regularly. When one or two roots start to push through the drainage holes in the bottom of the pot, cuttings are ready to pot on individually.

2 Gently tease apart the roots of the cuttings and pot up each one in its own pot. At this stage they should grow on well, without needing a plastic bag cloche, but keep them on a windowsill indoors, or in a cold frame.

Allow some plants to grow naturally *Seedlings of California poppies (Eschscholzia californica) just don't thrive if shifted to a new flowering position, so enjoy them wherever they spring up in the garden.*

around. But quite honestly it's easier to make a mini-cold frame with a crate and some perspex.

Transplanting self-sown seedlings in the garden

The majority of self-sown plants can be moved to new flowering positions with minimum losses. Transplanting them at dusk reduces wilting and gives them a little time to recover before temperatures rise again the next day. Water plants well before moving them, then dig them up with plenty of soil round the roots. Use a hand fork to do this, to minimise root damage. Dig the new planting hole so that it is big enough to take the root ball. Fill the bottom of the hole with water, allow it to drain, then lower the plant in, firming the soil back around its roots. Leave a shallow depression around the stem to hold water when you water the plant and direct it toward the roots. Water them in with water at ambient temperature, from a rain butt or watering can that has been standing in the sun for a few hours. Water transplanted seedlings regularly until they establish strong root systems.

Seedlings that resent being transplanted are indicated in the directory entry, and include love-in-a-mist (*Nigella damascena*), California poppy (*Eschscholzia californica*) and clarkia (*Clarkia unguiculata*).

THINNING AND TRANSPLANTING SEEDLINGS

When you have a lot of self-sown seedlings emerging in one spot, you may need to thin them out to give plants an equal chance to compete for space, light, water and nutrients. You can thin seedlings twice if you have the time and patience. Your first chance is when the second pair of leaves – the true leaves – emerge. This is incredibly fiddly but even these tiny seedlings can be transplanted carefully with some success – how hard you try depends on how greatly you value that particular species in your garden. (Discard very spindly or distorted specimens.) Watering the soil before thinning makes them easier to remove. Then thin again when the seedlings have formed small plants. If you have a lot to transplant, keep them in a plastic bag to stop them wilting until you're ready to plant them up in batches. All these points apply equally to seedlings that you have sown yourself.

Controlling pests and diseases

Slugs and snails

Slugs and snails love tender young seedlings and small cuttings. There are a few tips that are worth following to try to limit the damage they do. Use cut-down plastic bottles as individual cloches for seedlings and small plants (see page 14), but make sure you don't trap a slug inside the cloche when

you put it in place. Slugs are a lot harder to spot than snails and may be lurking under leaves or just below the soil's surface.

Traditional preventive measures include making barriers around plants that slugs and snails are deterred from crossing. Garden lore cites all sorts of materials to use to encircle plants – crushed eggshells, soot or sharp sand may (or may not) work in your garden. All of these are sharp, gritty compounds that molluscs theoretically find it objectionable to cross. Traps that lure slugs and snails include saucers of beer that they fall into and drown. Grapefruit halves, or simply small pieces of wood, present them with ideal hiding places, which you can then turn over and wait for the local bird population to come along and help themselves. More modern methods include a biological control based on a nematode parasite that infects slugs. This is watered into the soil, where the parasites invade and kill any slugs they come into contact with.

New research suggests that the time of day you water seedlings affects the chances of slug and snail attack. Trials showed that seedlings watered early in the morning were less subject to attack than those watered in the evening. When slugs and snails are a problem, anything is worth trying.

Using a mini-cloche *A cloche made from a cut-down plastic bottle can protect small plants from slug and snail attack. Then, once plants get beyond a certain size, they can usually shrug off the odd tattered leaf.*

Barrier methods *A ring of crushed eggshells can protect a plant from snail and slug damage but will need checking daily. Once rain has washed a portion of the ring away or birds have scattered it, the defences are useless.*

Grapefruit slug trap *A grapefruit half will inevitably attract slugs to shelter under it during the day. Turn traps over regularly and dispose of the slugs beneath.*

Mildew

Mildew is a common fungal disease that attacks
plants in hot, dry summers, covering their leaves
with unsightly gray patches. One tip is to cut off
all foliage down to ground level and give the
plant a really good soaking – at least a whole
watering can full of water, more if it's a big clump.
(Make sure you put the diseased leaves in the
dustbin rather than the compost heap). With any
luck, fresh new leaves will start to sprout in a
couple of weeks.

Rust

Rust is another fungal disease that can affect
hollyhocks (*Alcea rosea*), sweet Williams (*Dianthus
barbatus*) and mints (*Mentha* spp.). As soon as you
see orange spots on their leaves, cut off the
affected leaves and burn them. If the problem is
not too severe, this can be enough to contain it,
but if rust really takes hold, you'll have to steel
yourself and dig up the entire plant and start again
with new stock, preferably planted in a different
part of the garden.

Blackspot

This fungal disease affects roses, causing
characteristic black spots on leaves and stems. It's
not too serious for the plant, but it doesn't look that
good and can be controlled to some extent by being
tidy. Rake up infected leaves in the autumn and
burn them to stop the fungus overwintering. Look
out for black speckled stems in spring and prune
these out straight away before they burst into leaf.

CUTTING BACK A MILDEWED PLANT

1 Lungwort (*Pulmonaria officinalis*) soon looks
unsightly if powdery mildew takes hold. The answer
is to shear it – and other similarly affected species – right
back to ground level, clearing away and disposing of
every diseased leaf.

2 Then water the plant thoroughly. Within a few
weeks new disease-free growth should be visible.
It's a method worth trying on any particularly tatty plant
that is past its best by midsummer.

CREATING YOUR
FREE GARDEN

Creating your free garden

How you begin to develop a garden on a tight budget depends very much on circumstances. In a bare plot around a new house, you are going to start off heavily in debt to family, friends and neighbours, who will probably be only too glad to donate cuttings and portions of favourite plants. In an established garden that you've just taken over, there are bound to be areas that need improving or are sparsely planted, where you'll want to start work and add new plants.

By planting cuttings, seedlings and bits and pieces from friends' gardens, your own becomes a

Creating height *The grey-felted leaves and great spires of yellow flowers of mullein (Verbascum thapsus) add instant height to a garden.*

garden of memories and souvenirs – lily-of-the-valley (*Convallaria majalis*) from the patch by grandmother's gate, a cutting of rosemary (*Rosmarinus officinalis*) from the house where you were brought up, and magenta Michaelmas daisies (*Aster novi-belgii*) that remind you of a country garden you visited, each autumn as they skyrocket into bloom.

Instant maturity

In a bare plot, the aim is to get a garden going quickly and that is where some of the vigorous colonisers come to the fore. Use plants such as the plume poppy (*Macleaya microcarpa*), which grows 6ft (1.8m) tall and has beautiful, vine-like leaves, to make a framework that looks bold,

Simple ways to fill garden borders
Dividing delphiniums gives good results and increases stocks quickly. Use them to create colour and height in midsummer. The poppies in the foreground are natural self-seeders.

imposing and mature, while at the same time giving slower-growing shrubs and perennials a chance to get established. After a few years, they can take a back seat rather than a starring role, as new players push themselves forward. Other plants that will add instant height – and so instant maturity – include mullein (*Verbascum thapsus*), evening primroses (*Oenothera biennis*), foxgloves (*Digitalis purpurea*) and hollyhocks (*Alcea rosea*). These are all biennials, so if you are in a hurry, make sure you are getting last year's plants that will flower this summer.

Annuals are enormously important in this context too, especially species that put on growth at a rate of 0-60 in a matter of months and make a fantastic show until the first frosts. For example, annual mallows (*Lavatera trimestris*) grow very tall very quickly and bear masses of lovely hollyhock-like flowers in pink or white. Invest in a few packets of seeds – or family and friends may have saved some seed from last year that they could spare – and you'll have some annual species in your garden for life. Forget-me-nots (*Myosotis sylvatica*), nasturtiums (*Tropaeolum majus*), marigolds (*Calendula officinalis*), love-in-a-mist (*Nigella damascena*) and clarkia (*Clarkia unguiculata*) will all self-seed and come up year after year if conditions are to their liking. Try growing nasturtiums up a simple wigwam of hazel wands bound together at their tips.

A garden plant or a nuisance?

Some of the plants listed in the directory that follows will no doubt be regarded as weeds by some gardeners. They've all been chosen for qualities that weeds are renowned for: their ability to colonise ground fast, to make a big impact and to make more plants. You will have to decide on your own definition of what constitutes a weed, and so determine which plants would be a nuisance for you and which would not.

A lot depends on how a plant behaves in the microclimate of your own garden. A species can be perfectly under control when it is grown in shaded, dry soil and behave like a bullying invader in richer soil.

If you are passing on a plant that is vigorous, point people in the right direction. For example, qualify a creeping campanula by saying: 'You might like this for that awkward bank by your driveway – it covers bare earth very quickly'. Or if offering someone a root of pineapple mint: 'Don't put this next to your prize double-primroses unless you sink it in a bottomless bucket first'.

Controlling over-enthusiastic species

Once shrubs start to put on significant growth and perennials start to form substantial clumps, it may be necessary to curb the more vigorous plants that you planted for a quick framework and instant maturity, especially those that spread by creeping roots or runners. Equally, if you want to add a vigorous plant but have only limited space, there are ways of confining it before it gets a chance to outgrow its welcome.

Plants like mints (*Mentha* spp.) spread quickly, becoming tangled with other plants. One trick is to plant them in a bottomless container, with the rim sunk just level with the surface. This stops them spreading everywhere. After a few years, they may need digging up and dividing, as they start to resent being confined and lose their vigour.

With bigger species, you need to fence the roots around, again below the soil, so there will be nothing unsightly on view. You don't need to dig too deep. Use whatever you have to hand –

old roof tiles, wooden boarding – and create an invisible 'cage' for the plant. After a few years, plants will need lifting and dividing to reinvigorate them.

Or you can simply intervene before things get out of hand. To halt the spread of species like Chinese lanterns (*Physalis alkekengi*), for example, use a spade to slice around the plant where you'd prefer it to finish, then dig out all roots and stems beyond that point. If the worst comes to the worst, there's no shame in admitting defeat and digging out and disposing of an out-of-control invader – permanently.

Over-successful self-seeders

Letting plants self-seed is one of the easiest ways to fill a garden, but there may come a time when you say enough is enough. If your borders are bursting with showers of lady's mantle (*Alchemilla mollis*) – not to mention every gap in the paving and the gravel drive – and feverfew (*Tanacetum parthenium*) and ferny fronds of yellow corydalis (*Corydalis lutea*) are peering out everywhere, you have several options.

The easiest is to cut down flower stems before they set seed. Either wait until the flowers have faded before you clip them back, or cut plenty of fresh flowers for the house – Lady's mantle and feverfew are very pretty massed together in a vase.

Another option is to spot developing seedlings while still small and dig them up and pot them to swap or sell at fund-raising events. If the neighbourhood is saturated with certain species, you may have to harden your heart and weed them out or hoe them off. But there's a lot to be said for letting such species make great generous drifts of colour in the garden – they have so much more impact than single plants dotted here and there.

Creating a carpet of flowers *There are cases where so-called invasive plants can be a positive asset, creating a spectacular carpet in less than perfect conditions such as dry woodland shade – here colonised by wood anemones (Anemone nemorosa) and Welsh poppies (Meconopsis cambrica).*

Making a tapestry of plants

Many of the plants in the directory (see pages 42–141) are ground-cover plants. That is, they will quickly colonise bare ground, making a weed-suppressing carpet by covering up the soil. They are all similarly vigorous and, if mixed together in a border, can all hold their own against each other. Hardy geraniums, bugle (*Ajuga reptans*), sweet woodruff (*Galium odoratum*), the low-growing species of comfrey (*Symphytum ibericum*), hostas and mat-forming campanulas will all spread outward to form a closely woven tapestry of leaves and flowers without a gap of bare earth and with practically no chance of a weed pushing through. Just make the odd gap in the tapestry for spring bulbs, annuals like forget-me-nots (*Myosotis sylvatica*) and perennial hellebores or peonies (*Paeonia officinalis*). Then add foxgloves

(*Digitalis purpurea*) and loosestrife (*Lysimachia vulgaris*) for summer colour in the garden.

Hardy geraniums are very useful, since many keep their leaves all year round and some even colour up in autumn. They form satisfying, rounded clumps and even the seedheads add interest with their long-pointed 'beaks'.

This kind of border needs very little maintenance. You may have to intervene occasionally to stop the comfrey from overstepping the mark; when clumps of other species really do get too big, you can lift and divide them, but it's hardly even an annual task. You can let well alone for several years.

By digging up and dividing plants and using them elsewhere in the garden in a repetitive planting, you get a very cohesive look. Repetitive planting is undemanding and it's easy on the eye.

A swathe of forget-me-nots in spring
Use forget-me-nots (Myosostis sylvatica) as a patch of colour in their own right, as here, or grow them through through taller plants, so that they wreathe through their stems like a smoky blue haze.

A spring tapestry
Snowdrops, miniature daffodils, green-flowered hellebores, and spring cyclamen in a woodland setting make a spring tapestry that will evolve as the months pass – the snowdrops fading away while the bold spiky foliage of the hellebores becomes more dominant.

Plants that self-seed

Gardeners are always discussing whether plants will 'come true from seed', which, loosely translated, means whether seedlings will resemble the parent plants in flower colour and leaf variegation, for example. In a formal garden, or in one that has a carefully planned colour scheme, this question is of paramount importance. In a more naturalistic, informal setting, it has less relevance.

If you are starting with named seed from a reputable catalogue, then the flowers will be as described. But when you let these flowers set seed of their own, bees bringing in pollen from neighbouring gardens will introduce variation into the next generation of plants. So if you began with a display of pink hollyhocks (*Alcea rosea*) in your garden, you shouldn't be surprised if next time around specimens spring up that produce flowers that are a much paler pink or a shade of warm apricot. Forget-me-nots (*Myosotis sylvatica*) that set seed will always produce plants that are recognisably forget-me-nots, but they may have flowers of a paler blue, or mixed sprays of blue and pink, while love-in-a-mist (*Nigella damascena*) flowers can show some wonderful variations in intensity of blue.

Plants such as delphiniums come in a range of cultivars, as well as species, and while the species and certain cultivars produce seedlings that resemble the parent plant, many do not. To increase stocks of cultivars that don't come true from seed, it is necessary to propagate them by taking cuttings from the parent plant and potting them up, to be absolutely certain of getting a perfect copy.

Summer wildflowers *A random composition of rampant self-seeders – daisy-like feverfew* (Tanacetum parthenium), *magenta rose campion* (Lychnis coronaria) *and love-in-a-mist* (Nigella damascena) *– that have been allowed to flower where they will.*

Colour variations *The common purple foxglove* (Digitalis purpurea) *is the starting point for many of the coloured cultivars, so don't be surprised if self-seeded plants of named cultivars revert to the original purple species after a few generations. Conversely, the species also produces colour variations of its own, including pale pink and white.*

PLANT DIRECTORY

HOW TO USE THE DIRECTORY

THE PLANTS IN THE following directory are listed alphabetically by Latin name. When you are looking at the entry for a plant, be sure to fold out the extended back flap of the book cover. This will give you an instant guide to the planting symbols shown immediately below the plant's common name. You'll have all the information you need at your fingertips to help you decide where to plant it – every-thing from how tall it grows to whether it thrives in sun or shade and whether it is scented or not.

Each entry includes a short description of the plant and, in some cases, information on closely related alternative species that are equally easy to grow and propagate. This is followed by some brief planting advice, plus details on how to increase your favourite plants.

Ajuga reptans

Bugle

ZONE 3–10   15cm 6in   45cm 18in

These undemanding plants have rosettes of leaves, from the centre of which rise small spires of indigo blue flowers. Bugle is a wild plant and is ideal for wild, woodland gardens as it tolerates shade. Its creeping habit makes it a useful ground-cover plant, and it will quickly colonise bare earth. The wild species has been improved upon by growers to include varieties with variegated leaves or bronze, plus pink or white flowers. If you want ground cover in a hurry, go for bugle.

WHERE TO PLANT
Bugle grows happily in sun or shade in most soils. In sun it will flower earlier and more abundantly, and some of the varieties with coloured foliage need sun to maintain the colour.

MAKING MORE PLANTS
Each parent plant spreads by putting out runners – technically, stolons – each of which produces new plantlets that root where they touch the ground. It's easy to separate them by cutting through the runner to detach them from the parent and then replanting them in a new area of the garden.

CARING FOR PLANTS
Bugle is a very low-maintenance perennial, though, for best results, top-dress with sieved compost or leaf mould annually and try not to let the plants dry out in a long, hot summer. As they are grown mainly for ground cover, their purpose is to spread and block out weeds, and they are unlikely to get out of hand.

Bugle can be left to colonise shady corners, or give it a helping hand and shift plantlets to new flowering positions.

Akebia quinata

Fiveleaf Akebia

ZONE 5–9 · 3m 10ft · 3m 10ft

Akebia is a genus that certainly deserves to be better known. It has three member species that are all perennial climbers. The flowers of fiveleaf akebia are delicately scented. Very occasionally akebias bear fruits in autumn, rather like fuchsia fruits – tiny, thin sausages the colour of aubergines.

WHERE TO PLANT
Although they may prefer a sunny spot, they most definitely tolerate some shade and can even cope with a north-facing wall.

MAKING MORE PLANTS
Unsupported stems that scramble along the ground will root at various intervals, making it easy to increase stocks by taking advantage of the plant's natural tendency to 'layer'. Just snip between the rooted sections, then dig them up and pot them up. If you prefer, you can take cuttings in summer, but it's easier to work with nature and let the plant do the job itself.

CARING FOR PLANTS
Akebias need some support to grow up – either wires or trellis, or even a clothesline that they can twine around, though if you use the latter option, you'll soon find it competing for space with the washing.

Fiveleaf akebias flower in spring – these climbing plants will soon cover a bare fence.

Alcea rosea

Hollyhock

ZONE 3–9 | 3m 10ft | 60cm 2ft

The hollyhock is a quintessential cottage-garden plant. Tall spires of flowers in pinks, whites, yellows and deep maroon start to open in early summer and carry on well into autumn, with even the occasional bloom in winter in a sheltered spot. If your plants are not overly troubled by rust, leave the hollow stems all winter – hibernating ladybirds appreciate them. *Alcea rosea* is the species from which cultivars have been developed, including wonderful double varieties as frilly as a pompon. *A. rugosa* is a species native to the Ukraine and has yellow flowers and hairy leaves.

WHERE TO PLANT
Hollyhocks like a hot, sunny site with well-drained soil, with some well-rotted manure worked in. As they can easily reach 10ft (3m), they will need staking discreetly. Bamboo canes painted green are useful here.

MAKING MORE PLANTS
Hollyhocks set seed freely, and the two species hybridise to give lovely colours. Pink *A. rosea* hybridised with the yellow *A. rugosa* can produce a beautiful shade of apricot.

CARING FOR PLANTS
Hollyhocks are blighted by their tendency to succumb to rust, a fungal disease that disfigures the leaves with horrible rusty blobs. Cutting off affected foliage as soon as it appears helps to some extent. Try also growing the plants as biennials rather than perennials: dig up this year's plants once they've finished flowering and throw them away, rather than composting them, to avoid spreading spores; rely on self-sown plants for next year's flowers. *A. rugosa* seems slightly less susceptible to rust.

Yellow-flowered Alcea rugosa *often proves more resistant to dreaded rust disease.*

Alchemilla mollis

Lady's Mantle

ZONE 4–8 · 45cm 18in · 50cm 20in

The tiny yellow-green flowers of lady's mantle make it a favourite with gardeners and flower arrangers alike. They are produced in early summer and last for ages. As the leaves unfold in spring, they look like tiny pleated fans and are covered in silky hairs that trap the morning dew. Fully expanded, the leaves are almost circular, but with squared-off edges, and they retain their downy hairs. This is a plant that nobody should have to buy; someone in your neighbourhood is bound to have seedlings to spare.

WHERE TO PLANT
Lady's mantle grows vigorously in either sun or shade and isn't fussy about soil type. Plants form a low, soft mound of foliage, from which the flower sprays emerge, and are ideal for a front border position. They make good plants for the edges of paths or patios as they spill over and soften any hard lines.

MAKING MORE PLANTS
Lady's mantle sets seed freely and new plants spring up wherever they are happy. If the spot they choose isn't to your liking, these perennial plants can be easily dug up and transplanted. As clumps grow larger over the years, lift and divide to produce yet more plants.

CARING FOR PLANTS
Once you have enough lady's mantle in the garden, you can always cut off the flowers when they've finished but before the seed has a chance to ripen. If you're feeling thrifty, hang the stems in a warm, dark cupboard to dry and use them in dried arrangements.

Lady's mantle is a froth of yellow-green flowers all summer long.

Aquilegia vulgaris

Columbine

ZONE 5–9 — 60cm 2ft — 45cm 1½ft

The columbine has unusual flowers with an outer ring of petals that are elongated into elegant spurs that make them nod in the slightest breeze. The flowers can be blue, purple, pink or white. Columbines are another cottage-garden favourite and are useful for naturalising in wilder areas.

WHERE TO PLANT
The traditional columbine is a plant that tolerates dry soils and dappled shade, making it ideal for more awkward areas in the garden.

MAKING MORE PLANTS
Columbines are prolific self-seeders and hybridise freely with other aquilegia species. If you are planning a particular colour scheme for a border, then keep them well apart, or, safest of all, stick to one species or cultivar that is known not to vary in colour. New plants take two years to flower from seed.

CARING FOR PLANTS
Columbines can have rather brittle stems, so to avoid too many broken flower stalks be careful where you plant them: don't site them too close to a path, for example.

Columbines self-seed with abandon, sometimes with surprising results.

Arenaria montana

Mountain Sandwort

ZONE 4–9 · 15cm 6in · 50cm 20in

Starry white flowers above a spreading carpet of soft grey leaves make mountain sandwort a pretty perennial that is ideal for naturalising on a stony site or at the edge of a raised bed. It keeps its leaves all year long so is useful for adding winter interest. It looks rather like a saxifrage, but is actually quite closely related to chickweed – an irritating weed with nothing to commend it. However, if mountain sandwort proves half as good at colonising ground as chickweed, then it is twice as useful and far more welcome.

WHERE TO PLANT

Mountain sandwort likes a sunny spot and well-drained soil. When rock gardens were fashionable, that's where it was grown. Today it is more likely to be seen cascading over a retaining stone wall or in a raised bed or trough, or even as a container plant.

MAKING MORE PLANTS

In late summer, when the plant has finished flowering, lift the whole 'mat' and divide it into smaller clumps and replant. Cuttings taken throughout spring and summer will root quickly in water or can simply be pushed into the soil where new plants are wanted, with a high rate of success.

CARING FOR PLANTS

Trim and tidy plants in spring, but otherwise leave them to their own devices.

Masses of simple white starry flowers of mountain sandwort (top) soften the edge of a gravel path.

Aster novi-belgii

Michaelmas Daisy

ZONE 4–8 | 1m 3ft | 60cm 2ft

Michaelmas daisies bring a welcome splash of colour to gardens late in the year. Cultivars come in colours from deepest carmine through lavender to white. As well as the tall cultivars, dwarf ones have been developed that make good front-of-border plants. All make long-lasting cut flowers. As these perennial plants flower so late, they are best in mixed borders where they don't leave too much of a flowerless gap until they burst into bloom.

WHERE TO PLANT

Michaelmas daisies need a sunny spot and prefer good soil. Try not to let them dry out in spring and summer. Dwarf forms can be grown in a container and moved into a prominent spot when they come into flower.

MAKING MORE PLANTS

Michaelmas daisies positively benefit from dividing: you can do it every spring to increase stocks and invigorate old plants. When tackling tough, established clumps for the first time, you may need to insert two garden forks back-to-back to lever them apart.

CARING FOR PLANTS

The taller cultivars may need staking or surrounding with neighbouring plants that will disguise any sagging stems. Some of the older varieties can be prone to mildew, so check before you swap or receive pieces from neighbours that the variety offered isn't one of them. Michaelmas daisies are susceptible to tarsonemid mite.

You can rely on Michaelmas daisies to put on a show in autumn. 'Kristina' has white flowers that are ideal for cutting.

Borago officinalis

Common Borage

ZONE 5–10 · 60cm 2ft · 45cm 18in

The starry blue flowers of common borage are alive with bees all summer long, and the flower heads carry a mixture of furry buds and blooms.

WHERE TO PLANT
Borage likes a sunny, well-drained spot. The one reason you may fail to get plants coming up every year is if the ground is too wet.

MAKING MORE PLANTS
Borage is an annual plant, but it sets seed prolifically: so once you have it in your garden, it's there for life (more or less), unless you have planted it somewhere very unsuitable. You can move seedlings if necessary, but you will get better results if you don't.

CARING FOR PLANTS
Borage plants can be rather straggly and untidy. Try growing them up through low-growing roses – they will cover up any ugly bare rose stems. If you want to prolong the flowering season, keep cutting off dead heads, although remember to leave some flowers to set seed for next year's crop.

Common borage flowers are a traditional garnish for summer drinks and fruit salads.

Calendula officinalis

Pot Marigold

ZONE 6–10 · 45cm 1½ft · 45cm 1½ft

This is the flower that has started many children off on the gardening path, and with good reason – it is easy to grow from seed and tolerates the most unpromising soil and sites. Pot marigolds are members of the daisy family and have similar flowers. The original orange single-flowered species has been supplemented by new cultivars in shades of cream and yellow with double or semi-double flowers. Flowers and leaves have a characteristic pungent 'green' scent, which – like that of chrysanthemums – you either love or hate.

WHERE TO PLANT
Pot marigolds prefer unimproved soil – rich soil encourages leaf growth at the expense of flowers. They do best in sun, but will tolerate light, dappled shade.

MAKING MORE PLANTS
Pot marigolds do self-seed readily, but it can be worth saving some seed and sowing it yourself the following year, just in case anything goes wrong. If you save some seed, you can also make successive sowings in late spring and early summer to ensure a display of flowers right through until the first frosts.

CARING FOR PLANTS
Cut off the dead heads of marigolds to keep them from flowering, but don't forget to leave some flowers to set seed so that they can self sow and you can gather some seed to save for next year. Slugs graze on the young plants, but self-sown plants that have germinated in autumn generally grow quickly enough to shrug off attack. Blackfly can be a problem.

Pot marigolds flower so prolifically you need never be without a posy for the kitchen window ledge.

Campanula persicifolia

Campanula

 ZONE 4–8   1m 3ft   50cm 20 in

Campanula is a large genus of plants, all linked by their bell-shaped flowers. Some of the most useful ones are the low-growing, carpet-forming species. Although many of these can become invasive, their flowers – and often their leaves – are so pretty that you can forgive them. In any case, they are not difficult to root out and tidy up.

Campanula persicifolia spreads by self-seeding, and its rosettes of pointed, slightly leathery, green leaves are instantly recognisable. The leaves are rather like those of a peach tree, so you'll sometimes find it called the peach-leaved bellflower. The original species has large bluish flowers and there is a white variant *alba*, plus various double and semi-double cultivars.

C. portenschlagiana (zones 5–9) forms shapely mounds of toothed evergreen leaves and produces drooping sprays of deep purple flowers in summer. Of similar size, but with untidier habit, is *C. poscharskyana* (zones 3–9), which has paler purple flowers. This definitely makes a bid to smother neighbours but is easy to keep an eye on and control. *C. cochleariifolia* (zones 6–9) is yet another low-growing, mat-forming campanula that spreads

Campanula glomerata 'Superba' has clusters of typical bell-shaped flowers.

by means of creeping stems. It is invaluable for colonising areas of gravel or paving, or for draping old walls with a curtain of bells.

Of the taller species, *C. glomerata* (zones 3–8) has the reputation of being invasive. The best way to deal with it is to pick masses of its deep purple flowers for the house, then dig out the invading rhizomes with a trowel and pot them up to make plants for swapping or to stock a fund-raising stall. *C. punctata* (zones 4–8) spreads in the same way by underground rhizomes. It has pink, almost papery, drooping, bell-shaped flowers.

WHERE TO PLANT
Grow creeping forms in places where they can contribute useful colour and shape to stark areas such as gravel drives, concrete or stone paving, or bare walls. While the taller campanulas will flower best in full sun, some do well in dappled shade, especially *C. persicifolia* and *C. glomerata*. In general, they are not too fussy about soil.

MAKING MORE PLANTS
Rooted segments of creeping campanulas or rhizomatous species can be lifted and transferred elsewhere or large clumps can be lifted after flowering and then divided. *C. persicifolia* self-seeds readily, and seedlings are easy to move to a new position.

CARING FOR PLANTS
To keep creeping forms looking their best – and to maintain control, if necessary – lift them every three years or so, after flowering, and replant fresh growth from the outer edge of the clump, enriching the soil at the same time. Clip over large clumps after flowering, to tidy them up. Slugs and snails do not bother these tougher sorts of campanula.

Campanula persicifolia self-seeds abundantly and is a natural partner for old-fashioned roses.

Centaurea montana

Cornflower

ZONE 3–8 · 60cm 2ft · 60cm 2ft

The perennial cornflower is a typical cottage-garden flower, which fills the border with its blue, thistle-like flowers and furry, grey-green leaves. It spreads where it will, sending out tough roots and popping up in unexpected places. There is a white variant *alba*, which is far less vigorous and has a much more open flower structure. This perennial species is related to the annual cornflower *C. cyanus*, but is less trouble to grow as you don't have to sow it anew every year.

WHERE TO PLANT

Perennial cornflower blooms most freely in sun but does fairly well in light shade too. Set out new plants between autumn and spring, preferably on moist soil that drains well.

MAKING MORE PLANTS

Clumps can be lifted and divided after flowering or, at a pinch, in early spring, before they have really got going.

CARING FOR PLANTS

Once perennial cornflower has finished flowering, cut it right back and water it well. This will produce a new flush of healthy leaves and help guard against powdery mildew, to which it is prone in dry summers.

It's a good idea to stake perennial cornflowers to stop the flowers from flopping over.

Centranthus ruber

Red Valerian

| ZONE 5–9 | | | | | | |

60cm 2ft   60cm 2ft

Valerian is a common wildflower of chalk cliffs, especially on the coast. It is useful in the garden because of its long flowering season, from early summer right through autumn until the first frosts. Despite its preference for chalk, it makes the transition to other soils, provided they are not too rich. Its long tubular flowers lure both butterflies and moths, especially hawk moths, into the garden. As well as the common red species there are two variants: 'Albus' has white flowers and var. *coccineus* has flowers that are a much deeper red.

WHERE TO PLANT

If possible, try to mimic red valerian's native habitat and plant it in pockets of soil on an old wall or an awkward dry slope. It produces more flowers on poor soil but does flower elsewhere and is worth trying in different conditions in the garden.

MAKING MORE PLANTS

If it is grown in conditions close to the wild, red valerian self-seeds quite reliably. In more lush garden conditions, it may be safer to increase stocks by dividing existing plants in spring, as they come into growth.

CARING FOR PLANTS

Cut back flowering stems and you may be lucky and get a second flush of flowers. Where plants are grown on enriched soil, leafy growth is encouraged and plants become unwieldy and straggly. Dividing and replanting every few years will ensure a supply of plants with a neater habit.

White valerian, Centranthus ruber 'Albus', flowers all summer long with the minimum of attention.

Clarkia unguiculata

Clarkia

ZONE 7–11 | 60cm 24in | 40cm 16in

Although cottage-garden annuals clarkia (*Clarkia unguiculata*, syn. *C. elegans*) and godetia (*C. amoena*) are now botanically classified together, their flower shapes are quite different. The latter has larger, cup-shaped flowers, while clarkia has single, flat flowers with fringed petals. Clarkias come in shades of pink, scarlet, purple and orange, and have slightly reddish, brittle stems and narrow leaves. They are very easy to grow and make colourful border plants. There are a number of cultivars, which include single colours, double flowers and also a dwarf mixture, which produces plants just 12in (30cm) tall.

Godetias are a native California wildflower, which was first described by Captain William Clarke of the Lewis and Clarke expedition in the early 1800s, whose mission was to explore the west coasts of America. A few years later, plants were taken to the UK and Europe by the great plant hunter David Douglas, and they've been grown in cottage gardens ever since. They seem to be considered a little old-fashioned now – the sort of plant that your grandparents might have grown, perhaps in a row in the vegetable garden, but not necessarily an obvious choice today. But it's a reputation they don't deserve, because both species are ideal garden plants, especially for encouraging children to get involved, since they are quick and easy to germinate with spectacular flowering results.

The simple shape of godetia's blooms is a clue to their nearest relatives, the evening primrose (*Oenothera biennis*) and willowherb (*Epilobium* spp.). The wildflowers and some cultivars have dark, contrasting blotches at the base of their petals to attract bees and other nectar-loving

insects. Cultivars come in shades of salmon pink, orange, red and white, and plants tend tobe 12–20 in (30–50 cm) tall.

WHERE TO PLANT

Sow the seed in its final flowering position, as the seedlings of both species are tricky to transplant – the junction of root and stem tends to be weak. If you sow the seed too thickly, thinnings will sadly have to go on the compost heap. If you sow the seed in late summer, the resulting seedlings are hardy enough to overwinter and will have a head start for summer flowering. They don't mind a little shade and are not too fussy about soil provided it is well drained.

MAKING MORE PLANTS

Clarkia and godetias both self-seed under the right conditions but save some ripe seed to sow next year in case self-set plants fail to materialise.

CARING FOR PLANTS

For a good display of flowers, enrich the soil with a little leaf mould. Take care when weeding because both species have brittle stems with a tendency to break off at ground level.

Clarkia (C. unguiculata) varieties make long-lasting cut flowers as well as cheerful garden plants.

Convallaria majalis

Lily-of-the-valley

ZONE 4–9 · 15cm 6in · 45cm 18in

Lily-of-the-valley is one of the most sweetly scented spring flowers, with exquisite white, bell-shaped blooms. It likes to run wild in moist, shady corners and for that reason is often labeled 'invasive'. Less vigorous varieties include *rosea* with its pink flowers, 'Albostriata', which has white-striped leaves and 'Variegata', which has leaves striped with gold.

WHERE TO PLANT
Lily-of-the-valley needs damp soil with plenty of leaf mould or garden compost worked in. Ideally, dig plants in some time over the winter – though not when the ground is frozen – making sure the crowns are just below the surface of the soil. Water well.

MAKING MORE PLANTS
Lift and divide established clumps in winter while the plant is dormant, replanting divided crowns straight away or potting them up.

CARING FOR PLANTS
A winter mulch of well-rotted garden compost or, even better, leaf mould, will encourage plants to produce the maximum number of flowers.

Lily-of-the-valley can be forced into flower early for a sweet-scented winter treat.

Corydalis flexuosa

Blue Corydalis

| ZONE 5–9 | | | | 20cm 8in | 25cm 10in |

Blue corydalis is closely related to the common yellow species (*Corydalis lutea*): both have finely divided foliage that looks like the leaves of maidenhair fern. Yellow corydalis' habit of seeding into the tiniest cracks means that it can edge paths and walls with a great froth of foliage. It blooms practically all summer long, producing spikes of curiously elongated yellow flowers, followed by neat seed heads. If you feel reluctant to give such a common plant space in the garden, then look out for the blue species or for *C. cheilanthifolia* (zones 5–9), which has equally delicate foliage that is tinged with bronze as summer draws on, becoming darker still in autumn. Its flowers are a slightly deeper yellow. Blue corydalis was one of the most fashionable new plants on the market in recent years, and although it doesn't self-seed, stocks can still be increased fairly easily.

WHERE TO PLANT

C. lutea more or less chooses its own sites, from old walls to shady borders, but always in partial shade at the very least and never in full sun. *C. cheilanthifolia* will grow happily in sun or shade. *C. flexuosa* is slightly more demanding in that it needs moist soil.

MAKING MORE PLANTS

C. lutea and *C. cheilanthifolia* self-seed freely, probably producing far more plants than you need, but these are easily weeded out. *C. flexuosa* can be increased by taking off some of the dark red stolons it produces in autumn and growing these on in pots.

CARING FOR PLANTS

C. lutea and *C. cheilanthifolia* are undemanding species. *C. flexuosa* will lose its leaves over the summer if the soil dries out, though it will rejuvenate in autumn if conditions are right.

Corydalis flexuosa 'Père David' flourishes in moist soil, so try to ensure it doesn't dry out.

Crocosmia x crocosmiiflora

Monbretia

ZONE 5–9   75cm 30in indefinite

Monbretias are usefully late flowering, bringing a vibrant splash of colour to the border late in the gardening calendar. Their swordlike leaves also add shape and height to the flowerbeds. They are quick-growing plants and will fill out and transform awkward corners with their sculptural clumps. In some areas, they have escaped the garden and become naturalised. As often happens, some of the improved varieties are less vigorous than the original species, being slower to establish and less responsive to division.

WHERE TO PLANT

Monbretias will tolerate light dappled shade and prefer moist soil that is also well-drained. Use them to fill in gaps under leggy shrubs.

MAKING MORE PLANTS

Monbretias do set seed quite prolifically, but the seedlings can be infuriatingly slow to flower – two years is the very least you'll have to wait. For quicker results, lift established clumps in spring and divide – but don't do it too often. Wait a few years before dividing clumps again.

CARING FOR PLANTS

Monbretias can put up with hot dry summers, but do better if watered in drought conditions. They are hardy plants, but in severe winters will benefit from a protective mulch of straw or bracken.

There are hundreds of cultivars of montbretia – 'Jacknapes' has bi-colored flowers of yellow and orange-red.

Cyclamen hederifolium

Neapolitan Cyclamen

| ZONE 5–10 | | | | 10cm 4in | 20cm 8in |

Drifts of Neapolitan cyclamen naturalised under trees and shrubs make perfect ground cover for an area that is sometimes difficult to plant up. The species flowers in autumn, producing characteristic flowers with sharply reflexed petals in varying intensities of pink.

WHERE TO PLANT

Plant Neapolitan cyclamen in moist but well-drained soil. When digging up tubers always do so when the plants are 'in the green', that is, in full leaf. They will establish themselves far more easily than dormant tubers will.

MAKING MORE PLANTS

When the flowers have finished, the seed heads swell and the stems corkscrew down toward the soil, to deposit the seed. Seedlings form tiny tubers, which grow bigger every year. Neapolitan cyclamen self-seeds abundantly. If you can, leave the seedlings in place, so that the colony expands into informal drifts of flowers.

CARING FOR PLANTS

Give cyclamen a top-dressing of leaf mould or garden compost in summer before they flower. Let newly planted specimens become established for a few years before attempting to move them.

The flowers of the Neapolitan cyclamen are produced in autumn, before the leaves.

Delphinium

Delphinium

ZONE 3–8 · 1.2m 4ft · 60cm 2ft

Delphiniums are traditional herbaceous border flowers, their great spires of indigo, pale blue, pink, purple, white and creamy yellow filling the background from early to mid summer. You even get the chance of a second flush of flowers in late summer if you cut the stems right back to the base of the plant before they set seed and give the plant a generous watering.

The plants take their name from the Greek *delphis* or dolphin, a reference to the shape of the flower spur, which looks like a dolphin's nose, particularly when still in bud. The open flowers have an intricate 'eye' or 'bee' of eight inner petals, often a contrasting shade to the large coloured outer petals. When they are grey and fuzzy, they look just like an insect settled on the centre of the flower.

The Elatum group hybrids, descended from the native Himalayan species (*D. elatum*), produce tall, unbranched spires of flowers and are probably the most familiar garden delphiniums. Plants in the Belladonna Group are very easy to grow and are smaller, with looser, branched flower spikes that are very popular with florists and flower arrangers.

WHERE TO PLANT

Soil type is not important to delphiniums, as long as it is free-draining – they will rot away in wet soil. For best results, delphiniums must be in full sun – although they will grow in dappled shade, the plants produced are weaker and the flower spikes nothing like the great massed spires you expect. For good-sized flowers, thin the stems in spring: if a crown has twenty shoots, for example, nip out some so that you are left with perhaps seven or eight, which will then produce larger blooms.

MAKING MORE PLANTS

Take basal cuttings in late winter or early spring, just as the shoots come through the soil. Delphinium stems are hollow, so the cuttings must be taken well below the junction of crown and stem. Pot up the cuttings and leave to root in a cold frame, if possible. They should be ready to hold their own in the border the following spring. You can also try detaching young shoots as they appear in spring and growing these on as cuttings in a cold frame.

CARING FOR PLANTS

Slugs and snails can cause considerable damage when young plants are establishing themselves. Try traditional barrier methods or cloches to keep pests out, or copy professional growers and water the ground with a solution of aluminium sulphate (2oz/50g aluminium sulphate in a gallon/4.5 litres of water), an acceptable organic remedy. Delphiniums are prone to powdery mildew, particularly the Elatum group hybrids, so regular watering is essential in hot, dry weather. If petals look as if they've been nibbled, earwigs may be the culprits. Set traps among the stems – upturned flower pots stuffed with hay and set on canes. Earwigs like to use these as shelters, then you can empty the traps daily and dispose of the earwigs as you see fit.

Colourful spires of delphiniums are one of the mainstays of the summer herbaceous border.

Dianthus

Pinks

ZONE 4–8 | 28cm 12in | 23cm 10in

Pinks have been grown for centuries, and today there are around 700 varieties. Old-fashioned pinks have just one flush of flowers in summer, the more modern pinks flower freely. All plants have grey-green, pointed leaves that last all winter long and grow in low, rounded mounds.

WHERE TO PLANT
Pinks do best in light soil – heavy waterlogged soils cause plants to rot and die in winter. They also need full sun if they are to flower well.

MAKING MORE PLANTS
Take cuttings in late summer, choosing stems that haven't flowered. Hold the stem of the plant just below a leaf node, where the leaves meet the stem. Then gather up the leaves and pull gently until the shoot comes out. Called a 'piping,' this will root readily. Alternatively, sever the shoots just below the leaf node, stripping off most of the leaves before potting them up.

CARING FOR PLANTS
Pinch out growing tips in spring so that plants form a bushy shape, then cut off dead heads regularly, to encourage more flowers. After a few years, pinks can look leggy and untidy, so replace them.

Modern pinks flower prolifically all summer.

Dianthus barbatus

Sweet William

50cm 20in   23cm 9in

Sweet Williams are closely related to pinks, as you can tell from their flower shape and sweet scent. They have broad, flat heads densely packed with small flowers in a mixture of colours, from plain whites and reds to white flowers encircled with red, and red flowers with white eyes and edges. They look good in a mixed border and are ideal plants to grow for cut flowers. Some varieties have leaves that turn dark purple and crimson as the plant matures.

WHERE TO PLANT

Grow sweet Williams in full sun, in well-drained soil. If sowing from seed, sow in spring in a seed bed, then transfer the plants to their final flowering position in autumn. They will flower the following summer. To persuade them to bloom in their first year, start some off in a seed tray on a windowsill in winter and plant out the seedlings in late spring.

MAKING MORE PLANTS

Traditionally, sweet Williams have been grown from seed every year, as they are not very long-lived, but if you treat them as perennials and leave them in the ground, rather than pulling them up when they have flowered, they will self-seed and produce plants to replace the old ones as they fade away.

CARING FOR PLANTS

Rust and leaf spot can be problems. If you find signs of these, pull up the plants and start again with a fresh packet of seed, rather than risk spreading the diseases. A sprinkling of lime will improve plants grown on acidic soils, as they prefer chalky soil.

Sweet Williams make a dense carpet of colour in the garden. They are also popular cut flowers.

Dicentra spectabilis

Wild Bleeding Heart

ZONE 4–8   60cm 24in   50cm 20in

The wild bleeding heart is an ideal shade plant that flourishes in dappled light. In spring it produces delicate sprays of heart-shaped flowers above luxuriant, ferny foliage.

WHERE TO PLANT
Use bleeding heart to underplant shrubs but keep them topped up with leaf mould and well watered.

MAKING MORE PLANTS
Divide plants in autumn or at the end of the winter and replant straight back into the border, in soil enriched with leaf mould or garden compost. Bleeding heart will also self-seed readily. If you grow more than one species, and don't want it to hybridize, cut off the flowering stems before they set seed and propagate by division instead.

CARING FOR PLANTS
Slugs and snails can make short work of destroying fresh young shoots in spring, so see page 28 for advice on combating these pests. Although the plants are hardy, the tender emerging shoots can be scorched by frost and cold winds.

Dicentra spectabilis forms a compact mound that can be divided in autumn or late winter.

plant directory

66

Digitalis purpurea

Foxglove

| ZONE 4–9 | | | | 1.8m 6ft | 30cm 1ft |

The foxglove suits a wild garden or, at any rate, a wilder corner, where its self-seeding habit can be an asset. Its tall spires of flowers are produced in summer, and if you let the plants self-seed, you will get an interesting mix of shades of purple, pink and sometimes white. The foxglove is a biennial and flowers in its second year, after which the plant dies (though, occasionally, a vigorous plant will last a few years longer). By letting plants self-seed, you ensure a continuous supply of flowering plants. Other species that self-seed include *Digitalis lanata* (zones 5–9), which has creamy yellow flowers and is not as tall, and *D. lutea* (zones 4–8), with pale yellow flowers and glossy leaves.

WHERE TO PLANT

Plant foxgloves in light shade, in moist soil enriched with leaf mould or garden compost. You'll probably want to keep them to the back of the border because of their height. Any self-set seedlings are easily shifted when small.

MAKING MORE PLANTS

Leave the flowers to set seed and resist the temptation to cut down the dead stems for a couple of months. If you must tidy up, then shake the stems over the borders and you'll get a satisfying shower of fine seed that should produce plenty of plants for the following year. There's no need to cover the seed; it needs light to germinate.

CARING FOR PLANTS

Foxgloves are undemanding plants that seem to be left well alone by pests.

From the humble purple foxglove many colour variations have been bred. Some come true from seed, others gradually revert.

Dryopteris filix-mas

Male Fern

ZONE 4–8 · 1m 3ft · 40cm 16in

Most gardens have a difficult spot where nothing seems to grow, not even weeds. But this does not have to be the case: even if nothing grows there now, the male fern almost certainly will. Its fronds will brighten up the dreariest situation and, although not strictly evergreen, they usually retain some colour all year round, until the new shoots start to unfurl in spring.

WHERE TO PLANT
The male fern is the least fussy of all ferns and is a great garden specimen. It can tolerate dry or wet conditions and will come up year after year. Avoid planting it in midwinter when the ground is frozen. If planting at the height of summer, you will have to water well until it's established.

MAKING MORE PLANTS
The fronds produce small brown sporangia on the underside of the fronds, which contain seedlike spores. But these do not grow into new ferns – instead they germinate into a prothallus, a small, flat, seaweedlike growth (smaller than a fingernail) that develops sex organs. When conditions are wet enough, millions of free-swimming antherozoids – the fern equivalent of sperm – are produced, and these make their way across the prothallus in a race to fertilize a single egg, from which the new fern grows. Try collecting the spores by shaking the fronds over a tray of compost and then growing them on in a cold frame, or simply wait for nature to do it and move the resulting tiny ferns (sporelings) to a new site.

CARING FOR PLANTS
If you are planting in a very dark, dry corner, improve the ground first with a little leaf mould or fibrous matter to get the ferns started. Once established, they need no further help.

The male fern will grow where nothing else will and is invaluable for heavy shade areas.

Echinops ritro

Globe Thistle

| ZONE 3–9 | | | | 60cm 2ft | 30cm 1ft |

The perfectly round flower heads of the globe thistle are packed with tiny florets of an intense blue and are a favourite with bees. The leaves are grey-green and quite spiny, but the stems are relatively smooth, making them easy to cut for fresh or dried arrangements. *E. sphaerocephalus* (zones 3-8) can reach 7ft (2.1m), so make sure you have space for it before planting a cutting.

WHERE TO PLANT
Globe thistles are easy to grow and thrive on poor soils in full sun. Plant them on a sandy bank, for example, and turn it into a feature instead of a problem area.

MAKING MORE PLANTS
Take root cuttings (see page 25) from an established plant in late autumn when flowering has finished. Pot them up and, for best results, overwinter the cuttings in a cold frame, or simply divide a large clump in spring and replant portions in a new flowering site.

CARING FOR PLANTS
Aphids can be persistent. The only cure – if you don't want to use a chemical spray – is to cut off the affected flower stem.

The globe thistle in bud already has a blue sheen that hints at the flowers to come.

Erysimum cheiri

Wallflower

ZONE 7–10 · 30cm 1ft · 30cm 1ft

Bedding wallflowers are traditionally grown as biennials, sown in autumn for flowering the following spring. But why make extra work for yourself when these plants are actually hardy perennials? If you cut them back after the first flush of flowers, they will continue to flower all through the summer and will survive the winter to start all over again in spring.

Seed of *Erysimum cheiri* tends to be sold in mixed colours, including red, yellow, cream, orange and shades that are close to brown. Also look out for perennial varieties such as *E.* 'Bowles' Mauve' (zones 7–11), which, as its name suggests, has deep purple flowers, set against greyish green leaves. The Siberian wallflower, *E.* x *allionii* (zones 3–11), has blooms of searing orange.

WHERE TO PLANT
Don't enrich the soil before planting wallflowers or they'll make masses of leafy growth at the expense of the flowers. Choose a sunny sheltered spot, preferably with free-draining soil. In traditional bedding schemes, wallflowers are paired with tulips, and this remains a combination that's hard to beat.

MAKING MORE PLANTS
Wallflowers will self-seed in the garden, producing new plants to take over if the original stock starts to look worn and leggy. You can take cuttings in summer: to increase chances of rooting, always take them with a 'heel' of the main stem. Pot them up and overwinter in a cold frame, if possible, or in a sheltered spot before planting out.

CARING FOR PLANTS
Small seedlings are vulnerable to slugs and snails, so always sow more than you will need.

Bedding wallflowers come in a range of colours and are intensely fragrant.

Escallonia

Escallonia

There are many reasons to grow these small to medium-sized shrubs. In coastal gardens their ability to withstand gale-force, salt-laden winds makes them invaluable for sheltering more delicate plants, and they make good hedging everywhere. They offer interest all year round, with their neat, glossy leaves and their small red, pink or white flowers, which are produced in summer and often carry on into autumn, *Escallonia* 'Donard Seedling' is a vigorous variety with white flowers flushed with pink; 'C. F. Ball' is a good choice for seaside gardens and has red flowers.

WHERE TO PLANT
Escallonias appear to thrive in sun or shade, but do best on well-drained soil. Prepare the ground for new hedges with plenty of well-rotted manure and water plants regularly until well established.

MAKING MORE PLANTS
Escallonias root easily from cuttings taken in summer, but you will need to start them off in a shaded cold frame and preferably keep them there over winter.

CARING FOR PLANTS
There is no need to prune the shrubs unless you want to shape them or to keep a hedge in trim.

Escallonias make robust hedging from 5 to 10ft (1.5–3m) tall, depending on the cultivar.

Eschscholzia californica

California Poppy

ZONE 6–11 | | | 35cm 14in | 20cm 8in

California poppies are practically infallible plants, which are easy to grow from seed. They have simple, open flowers like wild field poppies but in rich, glowing oranges and yellows, to which breeders have added shades of cream, lemon, violet, pink and white.

WHERE TO PLANT
Choose a sunny site with thin, poor soil – any added humus promotes leaf, stem and root growth at the expense of the flowers. In their native California, the poppies grow wild on stony hillsides and roadside verges.

MAKING MORE PLANTS
California poppies self-seed freely, but the seedlings are difficult to transplant. If you want more control over where they appear, collect the seed yourself and sow it *in situ*, either in early spring for flowers later that year or in autumn for flowers early the following summer.

CARING FOR PLANTS
To extend the flowering season for as long as possible, cut off the dead heads regularly, but to get a supply of seed or seedlings for next year, stop doing this while the weather is still warm.

California poppies are extremely free flowering and blaze with colour.

Euphorbia characacias

Spurge

| ZONE 7–10 | | | | 1m 3ft | 1.2m 4ft |

Euphorbia is a genus that includes plants of every shape and size, but all have long-lasting flowers that are usually yellowy green and cup-shaped. The true flowers are tiny and usually lack petals but are enclosed by showy bracts. *Euphorbia characacias* flowers throughout spring; it forms a large clump and keeps its leaves all year round. *E. griffithii* (zones 4–9) has red flowers in late spring, and *E. cyparissias* (zones 3–10) has yellow flowers that turn orange as they age and leaves that turn yellow as autumn approaches; both die right down in winter. A biennial species, *E. lathryris* (zones 6–11), is something of a curiosity, producing flowers on tall, straight leafy stems. It self-seeds everywhere, but the seedlings are easy to identify and replant. In the right place – the back of a border, for example – it makes an unusual focus.

WHERE TO PLANT
Most euphorbias thrive in any situation, apart from deep shade, and prefer well-drained soil.

MAKING MORE PLANTS
Take cuttings of *E. characacias* in spring or summer. Wear gloves, as the milky white sap bleeds and can irritate exposed skin. Pot up the cuttings and overwinter in a cold frame or sheltered spot. Stocks of herbaceous species that die back in winter can be increased by division in spring. *E. lathyris* self-seeds readily, and the capsules explode suddenly to catapult seed far and wide.

CARING FOR PLANTS
Cut back stems of *E. characacias* after they have flowered, or set seed, to leave space for next year's flowering stems to develop.

The flower heads on mature plants of **Euphorbia characacias** *subsp.* wulfenii *can be up to 1ft (30cm) across.*

Fuchsia magellanica

Magellan Fuchsia

ZONE 8–10 | 1.5m 5ft | 60cm 2ft

Fuchsias are underrated in the garden. Most people tend to think of them as tender container plants for tubs and pots, but there are plenty of hardy ones, too. The taller species make good hedging plants and create valuable shelter for more delicate plants. Although they are deciduous, their twiggy framework can still filter strong winter winds. They are very free-flowering and really come into their own toward the end of summer, when many other plants are fading, and they continue until well after the first frosts.

Look out for *Fuchsia magellanica*, the best known hardy species, which has a ring of crimson sepals with purple petals hanging below. It also comes in variegated and golden forms, which are not as vigorous: 'Versicolor' has leaves splashed with grey and green; as its name suggests, 'Aurea' has narrow golden leaves.

Of the hardy hybrid fuchsias, 'Hawkshead' (zones 8–10) is covered with masses of small white flowers and makes an informal hedge about 4ft (1.2m) high in good conditions, while 'Lady Thumb' (zones 8–11) has pink sepals, white petals and contrasting pink stamens hanging down, it makes a low spreading bush about 2ft (60cm) high. If you let them set seed, fuchsias produce small, sausage-shaped fruits, which were once used for making jam.

WHERE TO PLANT

Fuchsias don't mind light shade – in fact, full sun can scorch leaves – and they will even flourish against a north wall. To make sure they are properly established in time to survive the winter, plant them in the ground from early to

The Magellan fuchsia is a vigorous hardy shrub; even if it dies right back in cold weather, it soon makes good growth the following spring.

midsummer at the latest. Magellan fuchsias can be grown in containers, too, but bear in mind that they are only fully hardy in the ground, as plastic or terracotta pots do not provide enough protection against frost.

MAKING MORE PLANTS
Species fuchsias will come true from seed, but it is generally easier to take cuttings, just as you would for named cultivars. Take cuttings in spring: if you do this before shoots have set flower buds, they will root far more quickly.

CARING FOR PLANTS
Tidy up plants in winter, but don't prune hard until spring. After a hard winter, Magellan fuchsias and hardy hybrids will die right back to the ground, so you'll need to cut away all the dead wood to make space for new shoots that will be appearing at ground level. To get a good-shaped bush and the greatest number of flowers, pinch out the tips of the sideshoots, so that these are forced to make more shoots all down the stem.

'Rufus' is a very free-flowering, hardy fuchsia that grows to around 30in (75cm) tall.

Galanthus nivalis

Common Snowdrop

ZONE 4–9 | 15cm 6in | 5cm 2in

The common snowdrop hardly needs an introduction. It is the first sign of life in the garden and a welcome sight toward the end of winter. It has plain white outer petals and inner ones tipped with green; its equally common cultivar 'Flore Pleno' has frilly double flowers with a faint but delicious scent of honey; the flowers of 'Pusey Green Tip' have green tips on both inner and outer petals.

WHERE TO PLANT

Snowdrops are native to woodlands throughout Europe. Aim to mimic these conditions by planting bulbs below deciduous shrubs and trees, so that they get sun early in the year when they are growing, but are then in dappled shade throughout their dormant stage, as the trees and shrubs above them come into leaf.

MAKING MORE PLANTS

Clumps of snowdrops increase in size naturally; the bulbs produce 'offsets' or miniature bulbs, below ground and some species set seed. To take advantage of this, you need to divide them regularly to give them room to grow and flower. Dig up clumps after the flowers are spent, but before the foliage dies back – the term for this is 'in the green' – then replant the bulbs immediately in their new flowering position. This gives them a far better chance of survival than if you were to dig up the dormant bulbs in the fall and transplant them, or if you buy dry bulbs from a garden centre.

CARING FOR PLANTS

Dividing clumps as above will ensure a good show of flowers.

In the right conditions, common snowdrops soon spread to form natural drifts of flowers and can be left to naturalise in a lawn, provided you don't mow it too early.

Galium odoratum

Sweet Woodruff

ZONE 5–10 | 15cm 6in | 40cm 16in

Sweet woodruff quickly covers bare ground, forming a low carpet of bright green leaves, arranged like the spokes of a wheel around the stems. In late spring it is smothered with clusters of starry white flowers. Strictly speaking, it is not scented, but if you cut stems and dry them, they develop the smell of new-mown hay and were used years ago for freshening sheets in the linen cupboard.

WHERE TO PLANT

Use sweet woodruff to form a weed-smothering carpet under taller plants and shrubs, as it grows quite happily in light shade.

MAKING MORE PLANTS

Plants spread quickly and the longer, straggling stems often send out roots where they touch the ground. Simply break off a few stems with roots attached and replant them, or dig up a larger clump for quicker results.

CARING FOR PLANTS

In mild areas, plants will retain their leaves over winter, but can start to look very neglected. It is worth shearing off last year's foliage before it sends up fresh green new growth – don't trim off the latter or you won't get any flowers.

The fresh flowers of sweet woodruff are scentless, but when dried they smell of new-mown hay.

Geranium macrorrhizum

Cranesbill

ZONE 4–8 | 25cm 10in | 60cm 2ft

Spreading ground-cover plants, such as *Geranium macrorrhizum*, are a gift for gardeners who are pushed for time. Not only do they need very little looking after, but they keep weeds at bay, too. *G. macrorrhizum* has typical five-petalled flowers, which are pink in the original species, though cultivars have been developed with flowers that are magenta ('Bevan's Variety') and pale pink with deeper pink veins ('Lohfelden'). Its leaves are strongly scented — an almost medicinal aroma, which you either love or hate — and, as an added bonus, they often turn red in autumn. Even the seed heads are attractive, with a long pointed 'beak' that characterizes hardy cranesbill geraniums and that gave them their common name. You can use the seed heads to add interest to an arrangement of cut flowers.

G. phaeum (zones 4–8) has flowers that are so intensely purple as to be almost black. It forms soft clumps of foliage, above which the flower stems nod and sway. *G. endressii* (zones 4–8) produces clear pink flowers all through summer and spreads by underground rhizomes – it often seems to disappear from its original planting spot and reappear elsewhere. It is very efficient at colonising new ground and is one of the plants you are most likely to be given by a neighbour.

This is just a tiny selection of the most common hardy geraniums, and you are bound to come across many more.

WHERE TO PLANT

G. macrorrhizum is an obliging plant, happy in shade or sun. It puts up with the driest summer conditions and never looks neglected. Use it as ground cover under trees and shrubs, in a border of low-growing plants or to underplant roses, or grow it in large tubs.

Geranium macrorrhizum *flowers from spring to early summer and has coloured leaves in autumn.*

G. phaeum is a shade-lover, while G. endressii tolerates either sun or shade.

MAKING MORE PLANTS
Many geraniums self-seed in the garden and some varieties hybridize to produce brand new flower colours – if you dislike where they've ended up, new plants are very easy to move. Species like G. macrorrhizum send out long stems that root freely where they touch the ground, as well as self-seeding fairly readily. G. phaeum self-seeds, but you can also divide large clumps at the end of summer after flowering. Dig up sections of G. endressii, which will root easily.

CARING FOR PLANTS
G. macrorrhizum must be one of the most trouble-free plants there is. Pests and diseases seem to leave it alone. To get extra value from them, try cutting species like G. phaeum right back to the ground after flowering and then water generously; you should be rewarded with a second flush of flowers. But don't do this if you'd rather the plant had time to self-seed within the garden. Nor should you try this with G. macrorrhizum, which has much woodier stems and would take much longer to recover.

Geranium phaeum *is one of a few plants that have near-black flowers, which are just saved from being monochrome by a tinge of deep purple.*

Helleborus orientalis

Lenten Rose

ZONE 4–9

30cm 1ft   30cm 1ft

The majority of lenten roses are hybrids of *Helleborus orientalis*, which has flowers in a great range of purples, plums, dusky pinks and white. They are bold spring flowers and bear blooms for a long period of time. Even when the petals fade, the horned seedheads look just as interesting – leave them in place, of course, if you want to increase your stocks by self-seeding. Commercial breeders have rigorous development programs to select the best-looking hybrids, but it can be just as much fun to see what your own plants produce. Finally, when the flowers are truly spent, there are still the leaves to consider – their big jagged outlines having much to offer the overall design of the border – especially as the leaves are evergreen.

Other easy-to-grow species to look out for in semi-wild gardens include *H. foetidus* (zones 6–9), the so-called stinking hellebore, which smells horrible only when you get right up close to it. It has drooping, green bell-shaped flowers edged with purple. *H. viridis* (zones 6–8), the green hellebore, has become popular in informal bouquets and, unlike the other two hellebores mentioned, is deciduous. The Christmas rose, *H. niger* (zones 4–8), is another member of the genus, with waxy white flowers and yellow stamens. To grow perfect specimens for Christmas arrangements, cover the plants with a cloche until you want to pick them to protect flowers from mud splashes and rain damage.

WHERE TO PLANT
For best results, hellebores need dappled shade, but provided you keep the soil moist and topped up with a mulch of leaf mould or well-rotted manure, there's every chance you can grow them in sun too.

Lenten roses come in shades of pink, plum and purple, with contrasting cream or white stamens and a pretty ruff of leaves.

MAKING MORE PLANTS

The species mentioned will self-seed, but it's better to leave room for a clump to become bigger by a combination of growth and incorporating nearby seedlings. Dividing clumps can be risky – it's safer to look for seedlings some distance from the parent plant (to avoid disturbing the older plant's roots) and then move these to new flowering positions while they are young. They take a couple of years to flower.

CARING FOR PLANTS

When flowers begin to emerge in spring, cut back the previous year's leaves of *H. orientalis*. This not only shows off the flowers to best advantage, but also reduces the likelihood of fungal diseases taking hold on the old leaves. Black spots are an early warning sign of disease – cut off the leaves as soon as you see any.

The Christmas rose blooms in midwinter, the flowers gradually flushing pink as they age.

Hosta

Plantain Lily

ZONE 3–9 · 60cm 2ft · 1m 3ft

Plantain lilies are fast becoming the plant of the moment, and new cultivars are being developed all the time. Some of the newest and therefore the rarest are commanding high prices, but there are plenty of old favourites, which gardeners are only too happy to share. Most plantain lilies are grown primarily for their foliage rather than for their flowers, which makes a ground cover that is almost impervious to weeds and that brightens up shady corners of the garden.

Leaves can vary in colour from plain green to lime-green, from blue-grey to almost yellow, and may be ribbed, puckered, shiny, or matte. The Japanese have valued this foliage for years and consider it essential to flower arranging; florists are beginning to appreciate it in the West, too. *Hosta sieboldii* has green leaves with a smart white edging and produces violet flowers at the end of summer; it is a fairly small species that grows vigorously. *H.* 'Invincible' (zones 3–9), as it name implies, is reputed to be less troubled by slugs and snails: it has olive-green glossy leaves and faintly scented lavender flowers. *H. sieboldiana* (zones 3–9) has heart-shaped leaves that are distinctly blue in tone and that are even more prominent in the variety *elegans*.

WHERE TO PLANT

As a general rule, plantain lilies should be planted in shade – full sun can scorch and damage leaves. They prefer a rich soil and do well even in heavy clay, provided you take a few precautionary measures. Before planting in clay, dig in a spadeful or two of grit or fine gravel, at the same time adding a generous amount of well-rotted manure or garden compost. Use plantain lilies to border a woodland path or to underplant shrubs and trees. The density of the

The golden variegation on the leaves of Hosta fortunei var. albopicta *tends to fade as the flowers form.*

shade will have a bearing on how well they flower, so if planting in dense shade, be prepared to appreciate them more for their leaves than their flowers.

MAKING MORE PLANTS

Plantain lilies are easily propagated by division, but leave newly planted specimens for a couple of years to establish themselves before attempting to lift and divide them. Do this in late summer, after flowering, or early in spring before the plants really start growing in earnest. You may find that some plantain lilies self-seed, but the plants they produce will be very variable – like a lottery!

CARING FOR PLANTS

In autumn, a mulch of garden compost or well-rotted manure will be much appreciated, as will the occasional watering can full of water in dry weather. Plantain lilies leaves are notoriously irresistible to slugs and snails, but resilience varies between species and cultivars – ask friends and neighbours for recommendations. Try traditional stockades of crushed eggshells, soot and sharp sand, or mini-cloches when shoots are just emerging in spring.

Hosta sieboldiana *has puckered green leaves and white flowers. It can tolerate some sun.*

Hyacinthoides non-scripta

Bluebell

ZONE 4–9 40cm 16in 10cm 4in

The native habitat of the bluebell is woodland, which makes it an ideal species for naturalising in borders shaded by deciduous trees or shrubs. As well as being blue, flowers can also be pink or white, and the petals curl prettily at the edges as they age. A sizable patch of bluebells creates an unbeatable blue haze, like woodsmoke creeping across the ground, and has an unmistakable honey scent.

Another common species, *Hyacinthoides hispanica* (zones 4–9) has thicker stems and larger flowers, which are held more upright than the characteristically drooping bells of *H. non-scripta*. Its one drawback is that the flowers are not scented. It is even more vigorous at naturalising than the native species, so when the ground is already thickly carpeted, cut off the seed heads or pick plenty of flowers for the house. If you grow both species, they will hybridise freely and produce plants with some features of each.

WHERE TO PLANT
Bluebells like dappled shade and moist soil that will not dry out too readily.

MAKING MORE PLANTS
Divide big clumps in late summer. If you are worried that the leaves may die back before then, mark overcrowded clumps with a cane – colour-code it with a daub of paint to remind you why it's there. Both species set seed readily, though it may take a few years for new plants to reach flowering maturity. They also increase underground by "offsets" – tiny bulblets that separate off from the main bulb.

CARING FOR PLANTS
Under the right conditions, bluebells need no extra attention to thrive.

Create your own mini woodland by planting a carpet of bluebells for spring.

Iberis umbellata

Common Candytuft

| ZONE 7–11 | | | | 26cm 10in | 20cm 8in |

Common candytuft is another disarmingly easy species to grow. There are two main species: *Iberis umbellata* is low-growing and has flat heads of flowers; *I. amara* (zones 7–11) is much taller and is sometimes referred to as rocket-flowered candytuft. Both species come in shades of pink, purple and white.

WHERE TO PLANT
Candytuft needs full sun to flower and will flower more heavily on unimproved soil. Sow low-growing *I. umbellata* at the front of the border and let it spill over a path. Taller rocket-flowered candytuft is better at mid-border.

MAKING MORE PLANTS
Candytuft will self-seed, but the seedlings are nearly impossible to transplant. You can exercise a bit of control by pulling up spent plants in autumn and shaking them so that seed falls where you want more flowers. Alternatively, of course, you can save seed and sow it the following year in early spring.

CARING FOR PLANTS
Clipping over *I. umbellata* after it has flowered may promote a second flush of blooms, but if these are produced late in the year, you may not get any ripe seed.

Flowers of common candytuft can be white, pink or lilac and may be faintly scented.

Iris germanica

Bearded Iris

ZONE 4–9 · 80cm 32in · 60cm 2ft

The *Iris* genus contains more than 300 species, from miniature rockery flowers to water-loving, poolside species. Some of the easiest to grow are the bearded irises. The species, from which many cultivars were bred, has sumptuous purple flowers and fans of upright, sword-shaped leaves. It flowers for a few short weeks in spring, and the unfolding flower buds have a tantalizing spear of colour before expanding like butterflies' wings. Hybrids available have increased the colour range to bronze, yellow, raspberry pink and cream flushed with blue.

WHERE TO PLANT

Bearded irises aren't fussy about soil type, provided it is well drained. On waterlogged soil, grow them in a raised bed to improve drainage. For best flowering results, plant them in a sunny spot – preferably a sheltered one, or you may have to stake taller varieties.

MAKING MORE PLANTS

Bearded irises are easy to grow from fragments of rhizome – take cuttings when the plants are divided (see below). The rhizomes need sunlight to promote flowering, so don't bury them deeply – leave a quarter to a half of the rhizome above soil level. Trim back any attached leaves and press in the roots, and the new plants should flower the following year.

CARING FOR PLANTS

To keep them flowering well, bearded irises need dividing every three or four years. In late summer, after flowering, lift the clump and cut away and discard the central congested rhizomes. Improve the soil with some well-rotted manure or garden compost, then replant with rhizomes from the edge of the clump. Wireworms can bore through the rhizomes, which then makes them vulnerable to rot.

'Pearly Dawn' is a tall bearded iris that blooms in late spring and early summer.

Jasminum nudiflorum

Winter Jasmine

ZONE 6–10 · 3m 10ft · 1.8m 6ft

Winter jasmine is a shrub with long, slender, arching green stems, and it produces bright yellow flowers in winter and early spring. The yellow flowers appear before the leaves (hence the Latin name *nudiflorum*) and often begin to open on the bleakest of winter days.

WHERE TO PLANT
Winter jasmine is not at all fussy about soil and is completely hardy.

MAKING MORE PLANTS
Winter jasmine practically propagates itself. Wherever a branch arches over and touches the ground, it will put out roots. This can then be detached and used to start a new shrub elsewhere. If you wish, you can encourage it to layer by pegging stems to the ground to encourage new root formation (see page 23).

CARING FOR PLANTS
Cut flowering stems right back to within a few inches of the base when blooms are spent, at the same time cutting out any dead wood. If left unrestrained, a mature winter jasmine can reach 10ft (3m) or more. Although winter jasmine is not self-clinging, it can be trained to climb a supporting structure – typically a wall.

Unpruned and untrained, winter jasmine can scale 10ft (3m) without any trouble.

Kerria japonica

Kerria

ZONE 5–9 | 3m 10ft | 1m 3ft

The cheerful yellow pompons of the double variety 'Pleniflora' are probably one of the best-known sights in spring. The main drawback to kerria is that once established, it can look untidy when not in flower – gardeners who are less than fond of it liken its leaves to nettles.

WHERE TO PLANT

Kerrias are tall, undemanding shrubs that grow happily in sun or light shade and in almost any soil type.

MAKING MORE PLANTS

Kerrias are easy to grow and equally easy to propagate. The shrubs produce suckers that spring up a short distance from the main plant. These can be dug up and separated from the parent plant, then sited elsewhere. You can take cuttings in summer and stems can also be layered, but this is the slowest method of propagation and is usually unnecessary. If a plant grows too large, simply lift it and divide it into smaller clumps, then replant.

CARING FOR PLANTS

If you have plenty of space, leave the shrubs to grow unchecked. If space is limited, you can clip them roughly into shape, but do so immediately after flowering or you will lose next year's blooms. Occasionally, take out some old wood right to the base of the plant, to improve its appearance. Sometimes branches die back to a leaf node after pruning and need further cutting back to remove unsightly dead stems.

Grow kerria as a free-standing shrub in all but the coldest areas, where it may need the protection of a wall or fence.

Kolkwitzia amabilis

Beauty bush

ZONE 5–8 | 1m 3ft | 1m 3ft

The beauty bush is smothered with small, pink flowers in late spring or early summer. The flowers resemble foxgloves and if you peer closely, you can see that they are, in fact, lightly freckled with orange spots. The rest of the year it takes a back seat, but makes a pleasing rounded shape and has small, pointed, green leaves. The variety 'Pink Cloud' is slightly smaller but just as floriferous.

WHERE TO PLANT
Beauty bushes are not fussy about soil type, but will flower best in full sun. If you are starting with a small cutting, think ahead and give it plenty of space, as a full-grown bush can be up to 3ft (1m) wide. If it looks lost with so much space around it, keep the gap filled with annuals until it expands to fill the space.

MAKING MORE PLANTS
Beauty bushes produce plentiful rooted suckers close to the parent plant, and these can be dug up and replanted throughout the year, but ideally in spring to give them the maximum time to get established before winter sets in.

CARING FOR PLANTS
Generally, pruning is not necessary, but if a bush gets very congested, thin out a few stems at ground level after flowering.

Orange and pink is not normally considered an ideal colour combination, but in the beauty bush it looks perfect.

Lamium galeobdolon

Yellow Archangel

ZONE 6–10   15cm 6in   45cm 18in

Despite its habit of colonising ground with surprising swiftness, yellow archangel is a useful species in the right circumstances. It will thrive in situations where nearly every other plant gives up. If you are worried about it stealthily spreading into more manicured plantings, then choose a less vigorous cultivar. 'Silberteppich' grows far more slowly, but it does less well in very dry shade. 'Hermann's Pride' is smaller and slower growing too, as is 'Florentinum', which has splashes of purple on its leaves.

WHERE TO PLANT
Put the unimproved species in the darkest, shadiest corner of the garden, but give less invasive cultivars the benefit of the doubt and plant them in a better spot, with better soil.

MAKING MORE PLANTS
Yellow archangel spreads by runners, which then root to form new plantlets. Dig these up and transfer as needed.

CARING FOR PLANTS
Keep an eye out for tell-tale signs of yellow archangel's silver and green leaves appearing in the midst of other clump-forming plants, and root them out before they establish themselves. To increase foliage for maximum ground cover, cut plants back after flowering.

Match yellow archangel's vigorous habit with a difficult habitat such as dry shade.

Lavatera trimestris

Annual Mallow

 ZONE 8–11   1m 3ft 45cn 18in

Masses of silky petalled, open flowers resembling hollyhocks make annual mallow well worth growing in the garden. The species has flowers of rose pink and there is also a white variety, 'Mont Blanc'. For such short-lived plants, they grow tall, strong and bushy and do not usually need staking. The closely related perennial shrub, the tree-mallow (*Lavatera arborea*) is free-flowering and easy to grow, since cuttings strike roots almost as soon as you put them in the ground – you can use them to build up a pretty, quick-growing hedge in a couple of years or so.

WHERE TO PLANT
Annual mallows need full sun to flower properly; the tree-mallow will put up with a little shade. Neither species is fussy about soil type. Give both plenty of room.

MAKING MORE PLANTS
Annual mallows self-seed readily and save you the bother once you have them in the garden. Seeds germinate in autumn – which is the ideal time to make a first sowing – for flowers the following summer. Take cuttings from tree-mallows any time during spring or summer and they are practically infallible. There's no need to worry about cold frames; just push a cutting into the soil and watch it grow.

CARING FOR PLANTS
The annual species needs no special treatment. If a tree-mallow becomes untidy and straggly, it can be cut back severely in spring, right to ground level, and it will leap back into leaf and flower with renewed enthusiasm.

Lavatera 'Bredon Springs' is a hardy, semi-evergreen sub-shrub that grows to around 6ft (1.8m).

91

Leucanthemum x superbum

Shasta Daisy

ZONE 4–8 · 1m 3ft · 60cm 2ft

The classic Shasta daisy is a fail-safe perennial that comes up year after year and flowers all summer long. Mix Shasta daisies in the border with poppies and delphiniums for a traditional look, and stake the daisies along with the other two species as they soon get battered by wind and rain. There are also some cultivars worth planting: 'Esther Read' has shaggy double white flowers with no discernible yellow centre; 'Bishopstone' has single flowers, but the petals are fringed.

WHERE TO PLANT
Although they flower best in full sun, they will accept partial shade. Shasta daisies tolerate most soils, but perform better on slightly alkaline soils, so add a little lime to soils that are definitely acidic. Working in some lime-rich, spent mushroom compost is an easy way to neutralise the soil.

MAKING MORE PLANTS
Shasta daisies very often self-seed, and you can also divide large clumps in spring. If you have planted one of the cultivars, dividing is the only way to make more plants, as very few seedlings of named cultivars resemble the parent plants.

CARING FOR PLANTS
Plants are usually disease and pest free.

'Esther Read' (top) is a popular double-flowered cultivar of the Shasta daisy. It grows around 2ft (60cm) tall.

Limnanthes douglasii

Poached-egg Plant

ZONE 8–10

     15cm 6in 20cm 8in

In the past, poached-egg plant has been a popular rockery plant, but now it is fast gaining status as a plant that attracts beneficial insects into the garden. Hoverflies in particular can feed on nectar from its simple open yellow and white flowers, which resemble poached eggs, and these insects are very welcome in the garden because of their larvae's appetite for greenfly.

WHERE TO PLANT
Poached-egg plant likes moist soil, but this must be well drained. As well as growing it at the edge of a border, or to break up paving and gravelled areas, many gardeners are now growing it alongside vegetables to attract hoverflies to deal with aphid infestations. Bees love the flowers too, so attracting them to the vegetable plot means beans, tomatoes and other vegetables have a better chance of being pollinated and cropping well.

MAKING MORE PLANTS
Poached-egg plant self-seeds prolifically, so be on the look out for new seedlings the following spring – they can be easily dug up and moved to a new flowering position. Once it's established in your garden, you have it for life.

CARING FOR PLANTS
When making an initial sowing of seed, make one sowing in autumn for early flowers the following spring, and make a second sowing in spring for flowers later the same summer.

Poached-egg plant's natural habitat is damp fields and open woodland, but it has easily made the transition to garden plant.

Linaria purpurea

Purple Toadflax

ZONE 5–8 | 1m 3ft | 60cm 2ft

The purple toadflax is closely related to the yellow-flowered wild species often seen colonising railway tracks and embankments.

WHERE TO PLANT
Purple toadflax tends to seed in sunny spots, but it still seeds if you plant it in a shadier site. Soil is not too important, though well drained is the best.

MAKING MORE PLANTS
Purple toadflax self-seeds with abandon and is shameless about crossing boundaries into neighbouring gardens. The seedlings are easily moved. The pink and white varieties are less prolific, and it is a good idea to save the seed of both and sow the following spring – if you have a cold frame, you can start it off early.

CARING FOR PLANTS
In an exposed site, plants might need staking, but it hardly seems worthwhile: if the stems get battered, just cut them down and you should get another flush of flowers.

Purple toadflax usually seeds itself so freely you can afford to cut plenty of stems for the house.

Lobularia maritima

Sweet Alyssum

ZONE 7–10 · 10cm 4in · 20cm 8in

Along with blue lobelia, sweet alyssum, with its froth of tiny white flowers, is a stalwart of municipal bedding schemes. The two of them are often planted alternately to edge flower beds with a band of blue and white, more often than not with a central block of red salvia planted behind them. However, it deserves to be more widely planted, as it will cheer up corners of the garden, and as a persistent self-seeder, will turn up in all sorts of places where you would never have attempted to plant it – between cracks in paving, even in the gaps in an old brick wall. The flowers are deliciously honey scented and also come in different colors: 'Royal Carpet' is a regal shade of purple, 'Rosie O'Day' is rose pink and 'Violet Queen' is violet, as its name implies.

WHERE TO PLANT
If you are starting from scratch, sow seed directly in the garden where you want plants to flower. Sweet alyssum prefers full sun and well-drained soil but is not fussy about soil type. Thin the seedlings when they germinate and replant elsewhere or offer to neighbours.

MAKING MORE PLANTS
Sweet alyssum self-seeds prolifically, so once you've made an initial sowing, you need do nothing else.

CARING FOR PLANTS
Shearing off the tops of plants will stimulate them into producing more flowers, but remember to leave one or two unclipped to set seed for next year's plants.

Sweet alyssum is a rather old-fashioned bedding plant that has a lot more to offer if planted in a mixed border.

Lunaria annua

Honesty

ZONE 8–10 • 75cm 30in • 30cm 1ft

Honesty is best known for its seed pods, which, when stripped of their dull outer skin, reveal shiny, silvery disks prized for dried flower arrangements or for adding splashes of light to autumnal flower beds. The flowers are pretty too, in an unassuming sort of way – like old-fashioned stocks or sweet rocket, but sadly without the scent (the one exception is the variety *Lunaria annua* 'Munstead Purple'). There are a few varieties in circulation: *L. annua* var. *albiflora* has white flowers, while 'Variegata' has variegated leaves splashed with white, and purple or white flowers.

WHERE TO PLANT
Honesty grows well in sun or light shade, provided the soil is reasonably good. Sow seed *in situ* in the garden at the end of summer and the seedlings will flower the following spring – thereafter they will do the job for you.

MAKING MORE PLANTS
Honesty self-seeds readily and seedlings are easily transferred to where you want them to flower or into pots to give to friends. You can recognise them by their toothed leaves, which are rather like nettles.

CARING FOR PLANTS
If you want to cut the seed pods for dried flower arrangements, do so before they are spoiled by heavy rain. If you cut them all down, you'll have to collect the seed. Peel off the pods' outer skin, save the seeds that fall out, and then sow them straightaway in the garden. If you pick the pods before they are ripe, when they are still green, the disks will retain that green colour even when dried – but you won't be able to use the unripe seed.

Lunaria annua 'Variegata' has leaves edged with white that bring a touch of light to a shady corner.

Lychnis coronaria

Rose Campion

ZONE 4–8			60cm 2ft	30ft 1ft

Rose campion has soft, grey felted leaves that make a stylish contrast to its clusters of crimson-purple flowers. Look out, too, for white-flowered forms ('Alba') and deep crimson flowered plants (Atrosanguinea Group), which are just as easy to grow. The wild species *Lychnis flos-cuculi (zones 3–8)* has slashed petals that give it its common name of ragged robin.

WHERE TO PLANT
Rose campion will flower best in full sun but is still worth trying in light shade. It tends to flourish on poorer, even dry, soil. *L. flos-cuculi*, must have moist soil.

MAKING MORE PLANTS
Rose campion self-seeds readily. Seedlings are easily identified by their distinctive leaves, and they are simple to dig up and move. Sometimes plants produce what look like plantlets along their stems. If you cut these off with a portion of stem and plant them, they often take root.

CARING FOR PLANTS
In hot, dry summers, mildew can strike. If you have plenty of plants, pull up diseased specimens; otherwise, cut them right back to soil level and water well (see page 29).

The wiry branching stems of rose campion rarely need staking in the border.

Lysimachia nummularia

Creeping Jenny

ZONE 4–10 · 2.5cm 1in · 1m 36in

Creeping Jenny is a low-growing, ground-cover plant. It will colonise a piece of ground with surprising rapidity, and you may catch yourself wondering why it is that slugs and snails never seem to bother creeping Jenny – but that is the secret of its success. It has cup-shaped, yellow flowers and tends to keep its leaves through winter, which is another of its virtues. There is also a golden-leaved variety, *Lysimachia nummularia* 'Aurea', which can add a splash of cheerful colour.

Yellow loosestrife (*L. vulgaris*) (zones 5–10) is a closely-related border plant with the same instantly recognisable yellow flowers. It has tall spires packed with blooms. They make lovely cut flowers too, if you don't mind their habit of dropping petals; the petals are used at the base so they fall off in a shower of star shapes. The plants make big, spreading clumps in the border, and it's always reassuring to see the first shoots break through the earth in spring.

Easy to confuse with yellow loosestrife is *L. punctata*. It looks very similar but really prefers a wet, waterside habitat, though if you are given a runner or two and don't have a pond or stream, it should still do well in moist soil. There is also a stunning dark-leaved loosestrife, *L. ciliata* 'Firecracker' which is well worth looking out for.

Less vigorous than the common yellow species, is the gooseneck loosestrife (*L. clethroides*) (zones 4–9), which has densely packed spires of white flowers with a curious twist in the stem, which resembles the sinuous curve of a goose's neck. If plants are grown in partial shade, the flower

spikes always turn toward the sun as it moves around the garden.

WHERE TO PLANT

Creeping Jenny is useful to break up areas of paving, on terrace walls, or even at the edges of ponds. Yellow loosestrife grows happily in sun or shade in reasonably good soil, but will appreciate watering in dry summers. Gooseneck loosestrife needs moist soil, or it will suffer badly and wilt in hot, dry weather.

MAKING MORE PLANTS

Divide yellow loosestrife or gooseneck loosestrife in spring to make new plants and replant straightaway in their new positions. You can easily dig up pieces of creeping Jenny and replant them as needed, or you can take cuttings and place them in water in the spring until roots form.

CARING FOR PLANTS

On windy sites yellow loosestrife may need staking. Creeping Jenny is undemanding. Dividing plants every other year, or yearly if they really get out of hand, will control their spread and improve flowering.

Creeping Jenny (L. nummularia) is a low-growing and extremely efficient ground-cover loosestrife species.

Macleaya cordata

Plume Poppy

ZONE 4–9 · 1.8m 6ft · 60cm 2ft

The plume poppy is a bold architectural plant, which can reach 6ft (1.8m) in a summer to make a spectacular display. It produces great plumes of creamy white flowers, up to 2ft (60cm) long, and has beautifully lobed leaves with soft, silky undersides.

The true species spreads very slowly, but plants sold as *Macleaya cordata* often turn out to be the invasive *M. x kewensis*, which can be a bit of a bully. If you want to confine it to a small space, take steps to control it before you plant (see below and page 34). If, on the other hand, you need something to fill a great blank space, then let it romp away. There is another vigorous species that you might come across, *M. microcarpa*, which produces interesting papery seed capsules.

WHERE TO PLANT

Because of its great height, the plume poppy needs to sit at the back of a border or close to a boundary unless you want to hack your way through a jungle.

MAKING MORE PLANTS

The plume poppy spreads by underground rhizomes, and new plants spring up a short distance from the original parent. These can easily be separated and dug up, to be moved elsewhere in the garden or passed on to friends and neighbours.

CARING FOR PLANTS

To keep the more vigorous species contained, dig a series of encircling trenches and stand old slates or tiles on edge in it before refilling, to make a barrier. Then plant the plume poppy within their confines.

The undersides of the leaves of the plume poppy are covered with soft, downy hairs.

Melissa officinalis

Lemon Balm

| ZONE 4–9 | | | | 60cm 2ft | 30cm 1ft |

Lemon balm has deliciously scented leaves with tiny white flowers hidden deep in the whorls of leaves. Bees love them, hence it is sometimes called bee balm. Look out for the variegated variety, *Melissa officinalis* 'Aurea', which has showy leaves splashed with gold.

WHERE TO PLANT
Lemon balm will flourish in sun or shade, in any soil, and will even make a show in every gardener's nightmare – dry shade. Plant it in spring or autumn and thereafter it will self-seed throughout the garden.

MAKING MORE PLANTS
Once plants are established, look out for self-set seedlings, which often have a helpful knack of coming up in awkward, uncared-for spots. You can also divide lemon balm to pass it on to friends and neighbours – just dig up a corner of a clump with some roots attached.

CARING FOR PLANTS
To keep the distinctive colouration of the variegated variety, cut down stems after flowering. This will, of course, prevent self-seeding, so you'll have to increase stocks by division.

Crush a leaf of fragrant lemon balm between your fingers every time you pass a plant.

Mentha

Mint

ZONE 3–10 · 30cm 1ft · 30cm 1ft

Mints can be loosely divided into culinary species and those that are equally aromatic, but inedible. Spearmint (*Mentha spicata*) (zones 3–10) has purply stems and narrow, dark green leaves, and a strong flavour. Apple mint (*M. suaveolens*) (zones 5–9) has hairy, round leaves, which make it look unappetizing, but some people swear it makes the best mint sauce. Moroccan mint (*M. spicata* var. *crispa* 'Moroccan') has pale green leaves that are distinctly puckered and is cultivated in its native North Africa for making tea. Moroccans steep a generous handful of leaves in a glass or teapot, so you need to grow plenty if you want to drink mint tea regularly. *Mentha* x *piperita* is another common mint that is good for tea drinkers.

Of the decorative garden mints, there is eau-de-cologne mint (*M.* x *piperita* f. *citrata*) (zones 3–10), which has the penetrating, fresh scent of the classic perfume and is useful for adding to potpourri or for scenting a bath. Ginger mint (*M.* x *gracilis* 'Variegata') (zones 3–10) has a faintly gingery overtone to its typical mint scent and has pretty leaves flecked with gold. Pineapple mint (*M. suaveolens* 'Variegata') (zones 6–10) has furry leaves that are widely edged with cream.

All mints have tiny flowers in shades of pink, purple or white, packed in whorls along the stems or gathered in loose spires. Bees love them and so, curiously, do flies.

WHERE TO PLANT
Plant mints in sun or shade, in reasonably moist soil if possible. If growing them as part of a

Many mints, including the strongly peppermint flavored Mentha x piperita, can be used to make mint tea, an infusion of leaves popular in North African countries.

herb garden, it can be a good idea to confine the roots, so that they don't colonise the whole bed, popping up in the middle of other species. Do this by planting them in a bottomless bucket or large pot, sunk in the soil to its rim (see page 34).

MAKING MORE PLANTS

Mints can be divided at any time of year to make more plants. Cuttings also root easily – if you keep a bunch of mint handy in a jar on the kitchen windowsill, it may well have begun to sprout roots by the time you are ready to use it. To keep a supply going over winter, pot up a few roots and grow them indoors.

CARING FOR PLANTS

Mints can develop rust, a fungal disease. In a mild infestation, cutting off stems and burning them (rather than composting) may be sufficient. If the rust overwinters in the plants, though, you may have to dig them out and dispose of the plants, starting again with new stock somewhere else in the garden.

Mints have a high rate of hybridisation and often produce 'sports' like these neatly edged leaves.

Milium effusum 'Aureum'

Bowles' Golden Grass

ZONE 5–8 | 30cm 12in | 20cm 8in

As well as being fashionable plants, grasses are becoming an indispensable part of the gardener's working palette of plants. Bowles' golden grass is an ideal introduction to ornamental grasses. It forms relatively low mounds, and its leaves, stems and flower spikes are all an astonishing shade of yellow, which is at its strongest in spring and in full sun. If the grass is grown in shade, the tone will be modified to more of a lime green. Typical grass flower spikes are produced in early summer, but after that plants tend to fade away as the temperature rises, but start strongly into growth again in the fall – a habit that indicates it is a cool-season grass, native to temperate regions of the world.

WHERE TO PLANT
Although its colour is strongest in sun, Bowles' golden grass actually does better overall in shade. Try planting it in woodland areas. It also needs moist soil.

MAKING MORE PLANTS
The grass self-seeds, but not at an overwhelming rate. Look out for seedlings in spring and transplant as necessary, or pot up and give away.

CARING FOR PLANTS
Water them regularly during their first year to help them become established, but once they are growing strongly, plants can look after themselves.

Grasses such as Bowles' golden grass have a long season of interest and need little maintenance once established.

plant directory

104

Muscari neglectum

Grape Hyacinth

 ZONE 4–10   20cm 8in 10cm 4in

There are several species of grape hyacinth, but this is by far the most prolific and has the darkest blue flowers of all the species. *Muscari armeniacum* (zones 4–10) is another vigorous species, which has tightly packed spikes of purple-blue flowers.

WHERE TO PLANT

M. neglectum has particularly untidy foliage, so try to mix it with something that can camouflage this. All grape hyacinths tolerate shade, but make sure that it is not too dense; in deep shade you will get no flowers.

MAKING MORE PLANTS

M. neglectum self-seeds freely, and the new plants will flower within three years. Bulbs of both *M. neglectum* and *M. armeniacum* also produce 'offsets', miniature bulbs, which soon mature into full-sized plants. To dig up self-set plants, or simply to divide big colonies, wait until summer when the bulbs are dormant.

CARING FOR PLANTS

Dividing clumps not only produces more plants, but improves the flowering power of those already established.

Grape hyacinths spread freely by a combination of self-seeding and bulb offsets.

Myosotis sylvatica

Forget-me-not

| ZONE 5–10 | | | | 30cm 15in | 15cm 6in |

As well as classic blue, forget-me-nots come in white and mixed shades – 'Victoria Mixed' include blue, white and pink. The botanical name *myosotis* comes from the Greek for 'mouse ear' because of the plant's hairy leaves.

WHERE TO PLANT
Forget-me-nots are self-sufficient plants, which thrive in most gardens but perform best in light shade and preferably on well-drained soil. They become straggly as summer approaches, so pull them up and let summer species fill the gaps.

MAKING MORE PLANTS
Forget-me-nots self-seed freely, but to make doubly sure, shake spent plants over the borders when you pull them up to make way for summer flowers. Seed that germinates in autumn will produce plants that flower the following spring. New seedlings are easy to dig up and transfer, or to pot up and give away.

CARING FOR PLANTS
Powdery mildew can be a problem if it strikes early in the season; but later on you can simply pull up the plants (perhaps a little earlier than you would have preferred).

Cut stems of annual forget-me-not in a delicate china teacup make a charming spring posy.

Nigella
damascena

Love-in-a-mist

| ZONE 6–10 | | | | 45cm 18in | 25cm 10in |

Love-in-a-mist is an old-fashioned cottage-garden annual that self-seeds with abandon – once you have it, it will spring up in all sorts of places you had not considered. The original species has blue flowers with a ruff of fine, ferny leaves around each one. The cultivated variety 'Persian Jewels' produces flowers in shades of pink, white, lavender and indigo; 'Miss Jekyll' has pale blue flowers, and 'Mulberry Rose' has pale pink blooms. After the flowers have been pollinated, the seed heads develop, swelling into interesting horned pods that are popular for dried flower arrangements. The seeds are aromatic and are used in Morocco to clear a blocked nose: the seeds are wrapped in a scrap of muslin, bruised, and then sniffed.

WHERE TO PLANT
Love-in-a-mist is a plant for sunny places and good soil. When first starting off, sow seed directly where you want it to flower. Thin out the seedlings to give plants a better chance to grow; sadly, you'll have to put thinnings on the compost heap, as they won't transplant successfully.

MAKING MORE PLANTS
Love-in-a-mist self-seeds readily, usually replacing current plants in the same flowering position, but also sending up seedlings far and wide. These are difficult to transplant and are best left where they are. Instead, collect the seed – easy if you hang up seedheads to dry in a big paper bag.

CARING FOR PLANTS
Cutting off dead heads prolongs flowering, but remember to leave a few plants to set seed for next year's plants.

As the flowers of love-in-a-mist age, the horned seed cases begin to develop at the center of the petals.

Oenothera biennis

Evening Primrose

ZONE 4–10 · 1m 3ft · 35cm 14in

Stately stems of evening primrose are topped with a crown of buds that open in succession, flowering from midsummer to autumn. The flowers are closed during the day but open at dusk to attract moths with their sweet scent. Traditionally, this plant has been regarded as little better than a weed, chiefly because it is so adept at self-seeding. The seedlings are easy to spot and transplant – or you can exercise a little more control and cut off most of the seed heads. But you'd be doing garden birds a disservice – a flock of goldfinches will soon strip a plant of seeds.

WHERE TO PLANT
Evening primroses must have full sun and well-drained soil.

MAKING MORE PLANTS
Evening primrose sets seed freely, and seedlings can be transplanted. As they are biennial, you may sometimes go a year without flowering plants. Seed that germinates in spring will not flower until the summer of the following year.

CARING FOR PLANTS
Plants are self-sufficient and not prone to pests or diseases.

The flowers of evening primrose attract both moths and butterflies into the garden.

Ornithogalum umbellatum

Star-of-Bethlehem

| ZONE 5–10 | | | | 25cm 10in | 30cm 1ft |

Star-of-Bethlehem forms vigorous tufts of grasslike leaves with a white stripe before flowering in mid-spring. The flowers are well worth waiting for – clusters of pure white stars with a green stripe on the underside of the petals – and they make pretty bouquets for a bedside table. But they can perform disappointingly in shade, and it can be frustrating to keep staring at a grassy clump where you'd rather have flowers. If conditions favour them too much, they can overtake the edge of a spring border, but people are usually only too glad to take some from you. The species *Ornithogalum nutans* (zones 6–10) is taller, with larger flowers, and brings with it a similarly vigorous reputation.

WHERE TO PLANT
Star-of-Bethlehem does fairly well in light shade but flowers more prolifically in sun. In shade plants produce foliage at the expense of the flowers. Choose a spot with well-drained soil. Plant them alongside species that will disguise their rather boring grassy foliage – forget-me-nots (*Myosotis sylvatica*) are ideal.

MAKING MORE PLANTS
Clumps of bulbs increase rapidly from a mixture of self-seeding and 'offsets' – miniature bulblets that separate off from the parent. The ideal time to divide clumps is in summer, when the plants are dormant. Use a cane to mark overcrowded clumps in case the leaves have died back by the time you're ready to divide them.

CARING FOR PLANTS
Dividing plants as above will improve their flowering rate.

Ornithogalum nutans is ideal for naturalising in grass as it quickly colonises open ground.

Osteospermum 'Lady Leitrim'

Sunny Ladies

ZONE 8–10 | | | | 60cm 2ft | 60cm 2ft

Although *Osteospermums* are native to South Africa, there are a couple of cultivars that seem able to withstand the coldest winter weather. All *Osteospermums* have daisylike flowers. 'Lady Leitrim' is a cultivar that has white petals with a metallic mauve underside, revealed when the flowers close up at night. *Osteospermum ecklonis* is white with blue-gray reverse.

WHERE TO PLANT
Try to plant them where they get sun for most of the day. Well-drained soil is best – you can improve the draining capacity of heavy soil by working in some well-rotted manure to open up the soil structure.

MAKING MORE PLANTS
The plants put down roots at points along the stems as they spread outwards, and new plants are easily made by cutting off a rooted stem. Give them away, or use them as a cheap way of filling garden planters.

CARING FOR PLANTS
Unlike tender varieties, these don't need frost protection and are not tall enough to need staking.

Plant osteospermums in the sun as the petals close up in shade or when the sun clouds over.

Paeonia officinalis

Common Peony

 ZONE 3–9   60cm 2ft 60cm 2ft

Peonies have been in cultivation for centuries and have been a cottage-garden favourite for longer than anyone can remember. The plants are incredibly long lived, and a clump flowering in an out-of-the-way spot may be all that is left of a house and garden long since gone. (Lilac trees are similarly long lived and another sign of habitation when all else has disappeared.) The common peony has single crimson flowers with contrasting yellow stamens and is slightly scented. It has a commonly grown double cultivar, 'Rosea Plena', which is packed with petals but is not fragrant.

WHERE TO PLANT
Plant peonies in full sun or dappled shade in rich, fertile soil. If your soil is poor, take the time to work in some well-rotted manure or garden compost before planting. Give them plenty of space.

MAKING MORE PLANTS
If you don't cut off the dead heads, *Paeonia officinalis* may (with a little luck) self-seed, as may 'Rosea Plena'. If they don't produce new seedlings, try collecting seed yourself the following year, then germinate it and grow seedlings in a cold frame. Otherwise, divide established clumps in the fall. Use a knife to minimize root damage and replant immediately, in soil enriched with plenty of well-rotted manure. They make take a year or two to recover and flower.

CARING FOR PLANTS
Sometimes clumps fail to flower well, and this may be the time to divide them and improve the soil. Top-dressing clumps with manure in spring can help promote flowering.

'Rosea Plena' is a cultivar of the common peony but, as with many improved varieties, it has lost the fragrance of the original species.

Papaver orientale

Oriental Poppy

| ZONE 4–9 | | | | 1m 3ft | 60cm 2ft |

Although the flowers of Oriental poppies are relatively short lived, they are spectacular: large plates of deep red, with a characteristic smudge of black at the base and a mass of sooty black stamens unfold all through summer. The buds are very appealing too, like furry green eggs, which gradually split to release the papery petals. Finally, the seed pods punctuate the border long after the petals have fallen. Along with the red-flowered original species, there are a range of coloured cultivars: 'Cedric's Pink' (sometimes known as 'Cedric Morris') has pale pink petals and retains the typical black smudges at each petal's base; 'Perry's White' has white petals with a crimson blotch at the base and a circle of violet stamens.

WHERE TO PLANT
Oriental poppies must have full sun and well-drained soil. They can collapse untidily after heavy rain and wind, so try to put some sort of support system in place before this happens – a framework of sticks is better than a single stake. As soon as the plants have finished flowering, they start to die back, so make sure they have neighbours to cover for them – perhaps some Michaelmas daisies just coming into bud.

MAKING MORE PLANTS
The poppies spread by underground creeping rhizomes, which make clumps easy to divide. For best results, do this after they have finished flowering. You can also increase stocks by taking root cuttings at the same time (see page 25).

CARING FOR PLANTS
Slugs and snails can polish off a row of seedlings overnight or graze new shoots back to soil level, so make good use of mini-cloches or slug and snail deterrent barriers (see page 28).

The generous flowers of the Oriental poppy can be the size of a dinner plate.

Phacelia tanacetifolia

Fiddleneck

ZONE 8–11 | 1m 30in | 30cm 1ft

Fiddleneck is an unusual annual with masses of fernlike foliage and flower heads that unfurl to form a shape very much like a new fern frond. You are now more likely to find it on a vegetable plot, where it is becoming more and more popular as a 'green manure' – a farming technique that's been adapted for the garden. Plants are grown to benefit soil that would otherwise be left bare, and are dug in at the end of the growing season to return nutrients to the soil as it decomposes.

WHERE TO PLANT

Choose a sunny spot on ground that has not recently been fertilized or improved. Sow seed directly in the ground in spring for flowers the same summer. If you know someone who grows fiddleneck as a green manure, ask if you could dig up a couple of plants for your border.

MAKING MORE PLANTS

Fiddleneck self-seeds freely, and seedlings do not suffer if dug up and moved while still small.

CARING FOR PLANTS

Don't try to do plants a good turn by digging in some manure or garden compost – they really do grow better in poorer soil.

Fiddleneck is a valuable bee plant and attracts them by the dozens.

Phalaris arundinacea var. *picta*

Gardeners' Garters

ZONE 4–9 · 1 m 3ft · indefinite

Gardeners' garters is one of the oldest cultivated garden grasses. It has boldly striped green and white leaves and a phenomenal ability to spread, which makes it a rampant ground-cover plant. It is one plant where the term 'invasive' may be used with some justification, so follow the technique suggested below to appreciate its clean, fresh colour scheme without undue worry. The cultivar *Phalaris arundinacea* 'Feesey' has leaves that are even whiter than the original variety and are tinged with pink when they are new. It also has the reputation for being marginally less invasive.

WHERE TO PLANT
To keep the strong variegation, plant the grass in full sun. Use it to help colonise awkward slopes, or mix it in the borders as a contrast to flowers. If the foliage starts to look neglected, cut the whole plant back to the ground and water well, and it will send up fresh new foliage.

MAKING MORE PLANTS
Gardeners' garters spreads prolifically by underground runners, which are easily dug up to plant elsewhere or to pot up until they form recognisable new plants.

CARING FOR PLANTS
To keep gardeners' garters where you want it and not where it wants to grow, use a spade to slice around the clump two or three times a year. Then use a garden fork to root out any runners beyond this area – pot them up to pass on to friends and neighbours or to sell at fund-raising events.

Gardeners' garters grows to 3ft (1m) in height and sends up even taller flowering stems in early summer.

Physalis alkekengi

Chinese Lanterns

| ZONE 5–8 | | | | 60cm 2ft | 60cm 2ft |

The papery orange lanterns that make this plant attractive are seed heads. The flowers are tiny, white, and almost unnoticeable. Apart from the original species, there is a naturally occurring variety, *P. alkekengi* var. *franchetii*, which has more shapely, pointed lanterns that are a more intense shade of orange. To dry stems for the house, cut them as soon as the seed heads start to change colour and hang them in a dry, airy place for a couple of weeks.

WHERE TO PLANT
Aim to put new plants in the ground between autumn and spring. Choose a sunny site; the soil is unimportant. If you know space is going to be a problem, set plants in a bottomless bucket buried in the soil, its rim level with the surface. To increase stock at a later date, you'll have to divide your original plant.

MAKING MORE PLANTS
Divide plants in winter when they are dormant and replant immediately. If a clump is threatening to overwhelm a border, chop all around the plant with a spade to the size you wish to keep, then dig up all surplus material and replant elsewhere or offer to friends and neighbours.

CARING FOR PLANTS
Chinese lanterns are resilient plants, largely untroubled by pests and diseases.

Chinese lanterns are papery seed heads, each with a berry inside. The orange colour develops as they ripen.

Physostegia virginiana

Obedient Plant

ZONE 4–8 | 1.2m 4ft | 60cm 2ft

Curiously, the flowers of the obedient plant can be moved from one side of the stem to the other, and when pushed into a new position will actually stay there. Its value in the border is its late flowering season, from late summer through to autumn. It is also a neat, upright plant that never needs staking and holds up well in changeable autumn weather. The species has pinky mauve flowers, and there are several cultivars, including 'Crown of Snow' and 'Summer Snow' (both obviously white), plus 'Variegata', which has pale lavender flowers and a creamy margin to the leaves.

WHERE TO PLANT
Obedient plant likes fertile soil enriched with garden compost or well-rotted manure. It flowers well in sun or dappled shade.

MAKING MORE PLANTS
Plants spread by runners and can spread quickly, so divide them in spring to produce new stock. If you do this every year, they should stay perfectly under control.

CARING FOR PLANTS
A mulch of well-rotted manure in early summer will boost flowers at the end of summer, especially in poorer soils.

Obedient plant is a native North American species, useful for late summer colour. The cultivar 'Vivid' has deeper pink flowers than the species.

Polemonium caeruleum

Jacob's Ladder

ZONE 4–8 · 60cm 2ft · 60cm 2ft

Jacob's ladder is an old-fashioned plant that takes its name from the pairs of leaflets arranged along the leaf rib like the rungs of a ladder. The original species has tall spikes of blue flowers, but over the years varieties have been developed to produce a range of colours. *P. caeruleum* f. *album* is white, not surprisingly; the flowers of 'Brise d'Anjou' have a noticeable violet tinge; while 'Lambrook Mauve' has lavender flowers and is named for Lambrook Manor, once the home of the British gardener Marjory Fish. The one criticism she reserved for Jacob's ladder was the flower spikes' habit of blooming from the top downward, so that the uppermost flowers are always finished by the time the lowest ones open.

WHERE TO PLANT
Plants will flower in sun or dappled shade and are not fussy about soil type, provided it does not dry out.

MAKING MORE PLANTS
Jacob's ladder self-seeds readily and the seedlings are miniatures of the parent plant, with the same ladderlike leaves arranged in a rosette. They are easy to transplant as needed.

CARING FOR PLANTS
Once you feel you have sufficient stock of these perennial plants, it's worth cutting spent flowering stems back to the ground to encourage a second flush of flowers. Taller plants may need staking in exposed sites.

Lavender blue flowers with contrasting golden stamens are typical of the original species.

Polystichum setiferum

Soft Shield Fern

ZONE 5–8 · 1.2m 4ft · 1m 3ft

Ferns are underrated and overlooked plants that are good for dealing with awkward sites in the garden. They can transform a gloomy city backyard or an area of dry shade under a tree. A border right up against the walls of the house can be surprisingly difficult to plant – the brick walls take up moisture and dry out the soil, and the overhang of the roof can seriously restrict the amount of rain such a border receives, but ferns will shrug off all of these conditions. The soft shield fern has very delicate, lacy fronds, which are finely divided. They stay green all year, which is a real bonus in a gloomy corner, and the emerging new fronds are densely furred with brown hairs.

WHERE TO PLANT
The soft shield fern is a little more fussy than the tough-as-old-boots male fern (*Dryopteris filix-mas*) in that it prefers a well-drained soil. It can also tolerate a little sunlight, though not full sun all day long. Dig in plenty of well-rotted manure before you plant it.

MAKING MORE PLANTS
When you spot what look like baby ferns sprouting from a frond, layer the frond by pegging it to the soil. The little plantlets will eventually strike roots and can be separated from the parent frond and replanted elsewhere. You may also find new ferns (sporelings) that have been produced from spores (for more information, see *Dryopteris filix-mas*, page 68).

CARING FOR PLANTS
Water well for the first year; after that, plants should be able to cope unaided.

The great advantage of the soft shield fern (top) is that it is an evergreen and keeps its finely divided fronds all year round.

plant directory

Pulmonaria officinalis

Common Lungwort

ZONE 4–8 | 25cm 10in | 45cm 18in

The common lungwort is one of those plants that has the ability to produce flowers in two separate colours on the same stem. It seems that the flowers are pink when they first open but turn blue as they age. The leaves are rough and bristly and are spotted with white or silver – in other species the leaves are even more decorative. *Pulmonaria saccharata* (zones 4–8) has leaves that are so heavily spotted that the spots can merge into a central splash of silver, with just a retaining margin of green to the leaf. The red-flowered species, *P. rubra* (zones 5–8), blooms earliest of all – in the depths of winter – and has plain, light green leaves and flowers that are a shade of coral.

WHERE TO PLANT
Lungworts do best in full or partial shade in rich soil that does not dry out. Plant them at the base of a hedge or mix them with small spring bulbs and, preferably, some taller summer perennials, which will detract from their foliage as it coarsens later in the year.

MAKING MORE PLANTS
Plants self-seed with abandon, so just dig up the new seedlings and replant where needed or pot them up to pass on to friends and neighbours. The plants produced are very variable, but that's all part of the fun.

CARING FOR PLANTS
Lungworts are very susceptible to powdery mildew. Cut affected plants back to the ground and water well (see page 29), and they should recover and produce fresh new foliage. This tip is also worth following if foliage begins to look ragged and the plants are in a very prominent position at the front of the border.

Pulmonaria 'Beth's Pink' has intense pink flowers and well-marked leaves.

Ribes sanguineum

Flowering Currant

ZONE
6–8

1.8m
6ft

1.2m
4ft

The brash pink flowers of the flowering currant are a familiar sight in suburban gardens in spring, often paired with boldly clashing yellow forsythia. They are two spring shrubs that everyone once had in their garden, but just because they have become overfamiliar is no reason to ignore them now. Flowering currants are cheerfully colourful early in the year, and a few bare stems brought into the warmth of the house will soon burst into flower. They have a pungent scent – some say the smell is just curranty, others that it's like cat urine, but you smell it only if you bruise the leaves. There are cultivars with flowers in varying intensities of pink, from 'Pulborough Scarlet' to pale pink 'Brocklebankii' to 'Tydeman's White'.

WHERE TO PLANT
The shrub puts up with all kinds of conditions, from shady walls to sunny hedges, and will suit all soil types. Plant them in a mixed hedge for a garden border.

MAKING MORE PLANTS
Take hardwood cuttings in autumn to make more plants. These are usually very successful and make strong little plants that can soon be planted in the border.

CARING FOR PLANTS
If you need to shape a bush, prune it immediately after flowering – if you do it later in the year, you'll trim off next year's flowers. Don't prune a bush just for the sake of it – birds are partial to the berries that follow the flowers. In old, established bushes, cut a few stems out right down to ground level to jolt the bush into new growth.

Flowering currant blooms early in the year; later on, birds appreciate its clusters of berries.

Romneya coulteri

Tree Poppy

ZONE 8–10   2.5m 8ft 2m 6½ft

The tree poppy has flat, open, poppylike flowers with crimped and pleated white petals and a central boss of golden stamens. The leaves are grey-green and finely divided.

WHERE TO PLANT

Good drainage is important, as is full sun. If your garden is exposed or in a frost pocket, choose a sheltered spot. Try not to disturb the soil around new plants in any way.

MAKING MORE PLANTS

If the tree poppy finds conditions to its liking, it will spread rapidly, sending up suckers some way from the original plant. Dig these up and sever from the main plant, then replant in a new position or wrap in damp sacking or newspaper to give to friends and neighbours. If the plant has not yet produced suckers, sit tight and wait. It's too much of a risk to dig the plant up and take root cuttings.

CARING FOR PLANTS

If you are starting off with a very small plant, it may be a good idea to give it a protective mulch of straw or bracken during the winter in cold areas.

The tree poppy flowers on this year's growth, so if you need to prune it, do so in early spring.

Rosa

Roses

ZONE 2–10 | 6m 20ft | 1.2m 4ft

There's a lot of mystique attached to growing roses, a throwback to Victorian times, when the aim of most growers was to produce blooms of exhibition standard, rather than a shrub that looked good in the garden. In fact, they are easy to grow, and the vast choice of roses available means that there is one for every possible garden situation. Although there are many different types of rose, they can be broadly divided into species roses and cultivated roses. Nearly all species roses have single flowers with five petals; with cultivars the only limit is imagination – there are double roses, those with quartered flowers, and flowers so packed with petals that they are almost spherical.

WHERE TO PLANT

Use roses like *Rosa rugosa* (zones 2–10) for dense hedging and windbreaks. Wild dog roses (*R. canina*) (zones 3–10) look natural scrambling through a boundary hedge of native shrubs, while species shrub roses, like the Scotch rose (*R. pimpinellifolia*) (zones 3–10), make big bushes that need very little attention, and are ideal for the back of a big border or a hidden-away corner, even in light shade. *R. glauca* (zones 4–10) can need a little support.

MAKING MORE PLANTS

Roses that do not have the dead heads cut off will go on to produce hips – some make such a colourful display that they are valued as much for their hips as their flowers. True species roses that are left to form hips will then give the plants a chance to self-seed. If the birds get to work on the hips, with any luck you'll end up with some seedlings in the garden sooner or later. *R. glauca* self-seeds readily in this way, as does *R. rugosa* and the wild dog rose (*R. canina*); the seedlings can be transplanted elsewhere in the garden.

Forget about techniques like budding and grafting, and try taking straightforward hardwood cuttings of your favourite rose.

Species roses like Rosa rubus, *a rambler, have a good success rate from cuttings or suckers.*

Species roses – that is, roses that are not grafted onto a rootstock – will often form dense clumps or send up suckers a little way from the parent plant. You can dig up and separate the suckers, or even cut through a corner of a clump with a spade, and then replant the divided piece with reasonable success. This is a particularly good method for increasing stocks of Scotch roses.

Commercially grown roses are produced by complicated techniques like budding and grafting, which are used because they achieve masses of stock from small numbers of plants. Taking cuttings uses up far more plants and so is less economically sound. In the garden, such considerations are irrelevant, and it can be surprisingly easy to take cuttings.

Take hardwood cuttings in autumn, choosing stems roughly the thickness of a pencil and strip off the thorns before following the method on page 21. The chances of success can be improved if cuttings are set out in pots in a cold frame rather than in a nursery trench, but the latter is still worth trying, especially with vigorous species roses.

CARING FOR PLANTS

Pruning is far too contentious a topic to cover here, but there are other tips to follow. Improving the soil with well-rotted manure gives new roses a good start in the garden. Another point well worth knowing is this: never plant a new rose exactly where you've dug out an old one, as it won't thrive.

Rosmarinus officinalis

Rosemary

ZONE 7–9

1m 3ft

1m 3ft

Rosemary is a Mediterranean plant, and its natural habitat is baking sunshine and fairly poor soil. It's been grown in gardens for centuries, and one romantic custom was for a bride to take a sprig of rosemary – very often together with a stem of myrtle – from her bouquet and then plant it in the garden. The spiky, evergreen leaves are just as aromatic as the flowers and have a pretty silver stripe on the underside that makes them popular for brides' bouquets and other flower arrangements. The common species, *Rosmarinus officinalis,* has purply blue flowers, but there are coloured varieties: *albiflorus* is white, as is 'Lady in White', while 'Majorca Pink' is purply pink. If you are taking cuttings from other variants, be sure to check whether they are hardy, as quite a few cultivars are not.

WHERE TO PLANT
Plant rosemary where you can appreciate its scent – by a bench or garden path or, if there's space, under the clothesline, so that it will perfume sheets as they blow to and fro across it. It's not fussy about soil and will even put up with a bit of shade, though it will flower less profusely.

MAKING MORE PLANTS
Rosemary roots easily from semi-ripe cuttings taken in summer, but the small plants do appreciate being overwintered in a cold frame before planting out the following spring.

CARING FOR PLANTS
Cut away any dead branches in spring and cut back any weak or spindly branches.

Evergreen stems of rosemary are becoming increasingly popular in flower arranging to add texture and fragrance to a display.

Salix

Willows

ZONE 5–8   15m 50ft   10m 33ft

There are many different garden willows. Species for hedging, such as the wild goat willow (*Salix caprea*) or the crack willow (*S. fragilis*) (zones 5–9), are very useful as they quickly form a windproof shelter to protect the plants within. Woven living screens are a good way of keeping vigorous willow plants under control – you may find courses teaching the technique in your neighbourhood. You can also pollard hedge willows to keep them under control.

WHERE TO PLANT
Nearly all willows are vigorous, fast-growing plants with enormous root systems that are notorious for interfering with underground drains, so think carefully before siting.

MAKING MORE PLANTS
Stems of crack willow placed in a bucket of water will form roots in barely longer than a week and can be kept in water for quite some time. They are so tough that even if the water freezes, they will survive. Hardwood cuttings root readily for most species.

CARING FOR PLANTS
If growing species for coloured stems in winter, cut the stems right back to the ground in late winter.

Many willows are grown for the fluffy catkins they bear in spring.

Salvia sclarea var. turkestanica

Clary Sage

 ZONE 5–10   1.5m 5ft · 1m 3ft

Clary sage is an extraordinary plant that sends up flower stems like branched candlesticks, from a rosette of hairy, dark green leaves. The stems are covered with typical sage-type flowers, enclosed by papery purple bracts that continue to look flowerlike long after the actual flowers have faded. As well as being a giant of a plant, it has, unfortunately a powerful and unappealing scent. Surprisingly, the plant's aromatic oil is used in the perfume industry and in aromatherapy preparations – presumably mixed with something more fragrant or else heavily diluted. It's a real talking point in the garden, as long as you don't get too close, or worst of all, brush against it.

WHERE TO PLANT
Plant clary sage in full sun, on well-drained soil, but don't grow it too close to a path, or worse, a clothesline. Mix it in with plants of a similar faded pink and purple – old roses, perhaps, and phlox.

MAKING MORE PLANTS
Clary sage plants tend to be short-lived and start to flower in the second year, like a biennial. They self-seed freely and can be moved to more convenient flowering positions or dug up and potted up to give away.

CARING FOR PLANTS
If planted on an exposed site, they may need staking. Aromatic plants are rarely bothered by insect pests.

Even after the flowers have faded, the coloured bracts of clary sage continue to create a good display.

Saxifraga x urbium

London Pride

ZONE 7–9 · 30cm 1ft · 60cm 2ft

London pride conjures up images of town and city gardens, where it obligingly edges the path, or cold plots, where it brightens up a cheerless corner. It deserves to be promoted and planted in a mixed spring border, where it can mingle with other plants. The flowers grow from rosettes of fleshy leaves, which stay green all year round. They look rather like exotic succulents, but are perfectly hardy.

WHERE TO PLANT
London pride prefers damp soil and shade. The closely packed rosettes make efficient ground cover, leaving little space for weeds to force their way through.

MAKING MORE PLANTS
Stems are easily detached with a sprinkling of roots and can then be replanted elsewhere. Clumps do tend to outgrow their situation, so divide to make more plants and keep the original in good shape.

CARING FOR PLANTS
Try not to let them dry out in hot weather. In early summer, cut off the spent flower stems to improve the plant's appearance.

Flowers of the genus Saxifraga are typically five-petalled and star-shaped.

Silybum marianum

Blessed Mary's Thistle

 ZONE 7–11   1.5m 3ft   1m 3ft

It seems perverse to suggest planting a thistle in the garden when a lot of time can be spent digging them out, but this thistle makes a show-stopping specimen in a wild garden. The leaves are marbled with white, which makes seedlings easier to identify and move to a safe position. The typical thistle flowers with a soft tuft of purple florets are delicately scented, if you dare risk getting close enough.

WHERE TO PLANT
Blessed Mary's thistles do best on poorer soil – manure and garden compost encourage roots and leaves to grow at the expense of the flowers. As they are seriously spiny, don't put plants close to a path or an area of the garden in regular use.

MAKING MORE PLANTS
The thistles self-seed readily and seedlings can be transplanted or potted up to give away, along with suitable warnings about the plant's final size and its spines. If you decide once is enough, cut off the flowerheads before they set seed and you'll have no more plants to worry about.

CARING FOR PLANTS
When seedlings are too small to be spiny, they may fall prey to slugs and snails.

If you dare get close enough, the flowers of this thistle are delicately scented.

Sisyrinchium
striatum

Sisyrinchium

 ZONE 7–8   60cm 2ft 60cm 2ft

The fans of sword-shaped leaves suggest that sisyrinchiums belong to the same family as irises, though the flowers are rather less exciting. *Sisyrinchium striatum* has creamy yellow flowers striped with brown, and it flowers for a long time: often a stem that looks finished will suddenly find a few more buds to open. Blue-eyed grass (*S. angustifolium*) (zones 3–10) is another self-seeder, this time with blue flowers. There are plenty of other species, but many are rock garden plants.

WHERE TO PLANT
Well-drained soil in full sun suits sisyrinchiums. Their strong evergreen foliage means that they can take a front seat in the border all year round, and not just when they are in flower.

MAKING MORE PLANTS
If you leave the flower stems to go to seed, they produce green, berrylike fruits, and the resulting seed can germinate in the most unlikely spots – in infinitesimal gaps between paving slabs on terraces and paths, for example. Seedlings can be difficult to wheedle out of tight corners, but they should turn up in easier places, too, where they can be dug up and transplanted.

CARING FOR PLANTS
Don't let plants get waterlogged or they will eventually rot. Although slugs frequently take shelter in the old leaves at the base of the plant, they do not seem to damage the plants.

Sisyrhinchium striatum is the commonest garden species with spikes of creamy flowers delicately striped with brown.

Stachys byzantina

Lamb's Ears

ZONE 4–9   35cm 14in   50cm 20in

Lamb's ears have leaves that are delightfully woolly and very comforting to stroke. They are silvery grey and the plant makes quite good ground cover, although it is not always dense enough to keep out persistent weeds like creeping buttercup. Lamb's ears lose their leaves in the winter in zones 4–7, and they may also lose their leaves in humid summer weather when the mean temperature rises above 15° C (62° F). The flower stems are woolly, as are the bracts surrounding the flowers. These flowers, if you can spot them, are typical of the mint family, having an upper and lower lip and being pale purple. Some gardeners feel that the flowers detract from the carpet of leaves. There is a non-flowering version of lamb's ears, a cultivar called 'Silver Carpet'. If you don't like the flowers, simply cut them off.

WHERE TO PLANT
Full sun and well-drained soil suits plants best. If they are grown next to a lawn, they do tend to creep into it.

MAKING MORE PLANTS
Their spreading habit makes lamb's ears easy to divide. Either snap off some loose stems and root them in a jar of water or dig a little deeper and pull out some ready-rooted pieces, then pot them up or replant elsewhere.

CARING FOR PLANTS
Sometimes powdery mildew can be a problem, covering the leaves with unsightly speckles (see page 29 for advice on mildew).

Stachys byzantina 'Silver Carpet' has no flowers at all, just a thick mat of woolly leaves.

Symphytum officinale

Common Comfrey

ZONE 4–9   1m 3ft   1m 3ft

Common comfrey is ideal for a corner of a wild, shady garden. It has drooping, bell-shaped flowers that can be creamy pink, or purple, and its foliage and stems are bristly. There is a low-growing species, *Symphytum ibericum* (zones 4–9), which has delicate drooping clusters of creamy white flowers, beloved of bees as they flower relatively early in spring. It makes tough ground cover in dry shade, but you may need to pull its questing tips out of neighbouring species before it colonises them.

WHERE TO PLANT
Comfreys can put up with most soils and conditions. Plant them where they won't overwhelm more delicate plants – use them to fill awkward corners and deep shade areas in the garden.

MAKING MORE PLANTS
Both species of comfrey mentioned spread rapidly and so are easily divided into rooted pieces to plant elsewhere or to give away.

CARING FOR PLANTS
Comfrey plants need no special care.

Symphytum ibericum is a resilient ground-cover species that flourishes in dry shade.

Tanacetum parthenium

Feverfew

 ZONE 6–10   45cm 18in | 30cm 1ft

Feverfew is a medicinal herb that has strayed into the garden proper. It bears generous sprays of small, daisylike flowers. There is also a golden-leaved variety, *Tanacetum parthenium* 'Aureum', and several double-flowered forms. Sometimes plants overwinter and last a couple of years, but do not rely on them to do so.

WHERE TO PLANT

Feverfew needs a sunny position and well-drained soil. Plant it so that its pretty sprays of flowers form a cloud around taller plants, such as delphiniums and phloxes, and at the base of hollyhocks, hiding their less-than-beautiful lower leaves.

MAKING MORE PLANTS

Both feverfew and the golden-leaved variety self-seed freely. Look out for the seedlings in spring and move them to their final flowering positions or pot them up to swap.

CARING FOR PLANTS

Cutting the flower heads off the golden variety is supposed to help the leaves retain their colour and appearance, but then, of course, you get no seed. Sometimes blackfly infest the flowering stems; the best cure is to cut off the stems and dispose of them.

Sometimes a fevefew plant will overwinter and last a season or two, but older specimens tend to get very woody and untidy.

Tanacetum vulgare

Common Tansy

ZONE 4–10 · 1m 3ft · 60cm 2ft

Common tansy is an old-fashioned herb that has fallen into disuse. The flowers were used to flavour puddings, and the aromatic leaves were dried and used as a moth repellent. In the garden, common tansy is a vigorous plant, quickly colonising new ground with its underground runners that send up shoots of the bright green, divided leaves. The flowers are yellow and button-shaped, like the centre of a daisy without the encircling petals. The naturally occurring variety *Tanacetum vulgare* var. *crispum* has even more finely divided fernlike foliage.

WHERE TO PLANT
Grow common tansy in full sun and fairly ordinary soil. If you are planting it in a limited space, take steps to confine it on initial planting by using one of the techniques on page 34. If adding it to an informal wild area, you can let it grow naturally among other vigorous species.

MAKING MORE PLANTS
As common tansy spreads in all directions, it's easy to dig up rooted sections to transplant to new areas or to give away.

CARING FOR PLANTS
Common tansy is more than capable of looking after itself.

Common tansy can be used as a safe flea-repellent for dogs, by rubbing the leaves into their coat.

Tellima grandiflora

Fringe Cups

ZONE 4–9 | 75cm 2½ft | 30cm 1ft

Fringe cups form neat tussocky clumps of hairy green leaves and, in spring, have tall stems of very unassuming flowers – small, greenish and bell shaped, with a minute fringe of petals. They are something of a floral curiosity: they smell quite sweet and make an intriguing addition to spring bouquets. Cultivars from the Rubra Group have flowers fringed with red petals.

WHERE TO PLANT

Fringe cups tolerate dry shade and are a neat way of dealing with ground cover in awkward corners, though if the shade is too dense, they flower less well.

MAKING MORE PLANTS

Both the species and its cultivars self-seed freely, and the seedlings quickly form good-sized clumps. Leave them where they are for all-encompassing ground cover, move them to new positions, or pot up to give away.

CARING FOR PLANTS

If clumps get too large, divide them in early spring, which is another way to make more plants. If the soil is in danger of drying out in hot weather, water them.

Fringe cups makes good ground cover for shady spots.

Tiarella
cordifolia

Foam Flower

ZONE 3–9 · 25cm 10in · 1m 3ft

Tellima and Tiarella are often confused, not just by gardeners but by nurseries too – perhaps because they are both good ground-cover plants for shade. Foam flower tends to form a carpet of leaves rather than tussocks and has far more small, starry, white flowers carried in dense spikes. Breeders have created cultivars and hybrids with interesting foliage and coloured flowers. 'Eco Red Heart' has leaves with distinct red centers and fluffy pink flowers, while 'Glossy' has shiny leaves but retains the original white flowers.

WHERE TO PLANT
Foam flower is a native woodland species, so plant it in a similar situation in the garden, under deciduous trees and shrubs, so that the plants get a little sunlight at the beginning of the year.

MAKING MORE PLANTS
When plants begin to spread beyond their bounds, lift and divide them, either in autumn or spring. Replant pieces immediately or pot up and pass on to friends and neighbours.

CARING FOR PLANTS
A spring or autumn mulch of leaf mould will mimic woodland conditions and improve growth.

In spring Tiarella 'Tiger Stripe' bears spires of flowers with boldly contrasting stamens.

Tropaeolum majus

Common Nasturtium

ZONE 8–11 | 1.8m 6ft | 2m 7ft

Common nasturtiums are easy-to-grow cottage-garden favourites that can be grown either as trailing plants or trained against a trellis to make a quick – if temporary – screen. The flowers come in a bewildering choice of colours and styles – there are spurred flowers, singles, and doubles, in shades of red, yellow, orange, rich brown, pink and tangerine.

WHERE TO PLANT

When sowing initially, do so directly in the ground where you want the plants to flower, as seedlings are difficult to transplant successfully. Like many annuals, nasturtiums do best in poor soil. They tolerate a little light shade.

MAKING MORE PLANTS

Common nasturtiums self-seed fairly reliably, but the seedlings resent being moved. To make sure you get plants where you want them, save some seed and sow it the following spring.

CARING FOR PLANTS

Blackfly can be a real nuisance. Try washing them off with soapy water or cutting off afflicted stems. Or send off for a supply of live ladybirds and hope they'll get to work quickly.

Common nasturtiums come in glorious colours and some have variegated leaves.

Verbascum thapsus

Mullein

Mullein often turns up uninvited in gardens, in areas where it is a common wildflower, but it is far from unwelcome. In its first year it builds up a rosette of soft grey furry leaves and in the second year it sends up great woolly towering stems, which can reach 6ft (1.8m) and which are packed with yellow flowers. Mullein is efficient at self-seeding, as are garden species of mullein, such as *Verbascum chaixii* (zones 5–10), which has yellow flowers with contrasting pink stamens.

WHERE TO PLANT

Make a focal point of mullein because of its great height. It needs full sun, so bear this in mind when moving a seedling. The smaller garden species can form part of a mixed border, again in full sun and on reasonable soil.

MAKING MORE PLANTS

Both mullein and garden species self-seed freely, and the seedlings are easy to transplant when young, unless they've rooted between paving stones, on terraces, or in brick paths, in which case you may have to give up any attempt to shift them. When you cut down dead stems, shake them over the borders to give every bit of seed the chance to germinate.

CARING FOR PLANTS

Both the wildflower and the garden species are a food plant for caterpillars in summer, and tend to get tattered by slugs and snails in spring. Garden species may need staking in bad weather, but the wild mullein is usually robust enough to stay upright.

Verbascum bombyciferum is very similar to the wild species but has flowers of a more intense yellow and multi-branched stems.

Vinca minor

Lesser Periwinkle

ZONE 4–9   60cm 2ft   60cm 2ft

Periwinkle is a useful ground-cover for dry shade. One of the most commonly grown varieties is *Vinca minor* 'Alba Variegata', which has leaves edged and splashed with yellow and retains its leaves all year round. It has simple white flowers in spring and summer, and sometimes a freak bloom in winter. *V. minor* is hardly significantly smaller than *V. major* (zones 7–10), but the latter can be a bit too vigorous for most gardens. *V. minor* comes in many more varieties which are mostly defined by variations in flowers rather than foliage.

WHERE TO PLANT

If it's the flowers of periwinkles that you admire, you need to plant them in a sunnier spot than if you merely want to use them as shady ground-cover plants. You will get some flowers in shade, but they are few and far between.

MAKING MORE PLANTS

Periwinkles layer naturally: where trailing stems touch the ground they very often root. Simply dig up and separate these rooted sections and replant them elsewhere or give them away.

CARING FOR PLANTS

To keep plants under control and improve the foliage, cut them back to the ground in spring.

Periwinkle can be a useful plant in awkward sites such as the dry ground at the base of a wall.

Viola odorata

Sweet Violet

ZONE 5–10 10cm 4in 30cm 1ft

If you have masses of violets in the garden, you can indulge yourself and pick tiny nosegays to balance in egg cups to grace the breakfast table or brighten up a desk. The more you pick, the more flowers they will produce in the race to set seed. There are several species of violet, and books warn that the common violet (*Viola riviniana*) is invasive, but who could object to being overrun with violets? Their dense clumps, studded with rich purple flowers, are a cheerful sight in spring.

WHERE TO PLANT
Mix violets with other woodland flowers for a natural wild corner – bluebells, primroses and snowdrops are ideal. More often than not, violets will choose their own spot – springing up in the gaps on a brick path or around the front door. If you can't get a clump from friends or neighbours, send for seed from a wildflower specialist.

MAKING MORE PLANTS
Some violet species spread by self-layering, the stems rooting easily where they touch the ground, which is how they form great spreading clumps. *V. riviniana* spreads by producing adventitious shoots from its roots. Either dig up sections from the edge of a clump or lift the whole clump and divide it in the autumn. Plants may also self-seed, and cut stems may root in water in summer.

CARING FOR PLANTS
As the summer goes on, the leaves coarsen and can begin to look tired, and it is worth cutting them back to encourage fresh growth.

Sweet violet is, as its name suggests, the most fragrant of all violets. It sometimes flowers again in autumn.

Viola tricolor

Heartsease

ZONE 4–10 | 10cm 4in | 15cm 6in

Heartsease is the true wild pansy, the ancestor of the exotic pansies we grow today. It often pops up in gardens, seeding around so that you never know where it will turn up next. Even in the wild species, flower colour can vary, but the top two petals are often purple, those at the side whitish, and the lower petals yellow. Common pansies (*Viola x wittrockiana*) come in a vast range of colours – many are sold as series or mixes. 'Super Chalon Giants' have ruffled petals in shades of red, yellow and purple; while 'Joker Light Blue' are single-coloured blue flowers with white central markings.

WHERE TO PLANT
Plant heartsease in well-drained soil in sun or light shade and thereafter let it seed where it will. Common pansies can be grown in borders or tubs, wherever you want to see their cheerful faces: try to keep them in full sun or they may go leggy.

MAKING MORE PLANTS
Heartsease self-seeds freely, and plants often have a knack of appearing just where they look prettiest. Common pansies self-seed too, but do not necessarily come true to the type you originally planted.

CARING FOR PLANTS
Cutting off dead heads prolongs the flowering season, but judge it carefully or you won't have any seed heads for plants to self-seed. Although common pansies can be grown as perennials, they become so leggy and sprawling that it's best to start afresh each year with new seedlings.

The original heartsease's three-colour flowers are here mixed with some of the many hybrids.

Weigela florida

Weigela

ZONE
5–8

2m
6½ft

1m
3ft

Weigela shrubs are easy to grow and flower reliably every spring, with masses of foxglove-shaped flowers.

WHERE TO PLANT

Choose a sunny site or one that is only partially shaded and on well-drained soil. Either mix in a border with larger herbaceous perennials, or plant a spring hedge with other old favourites, such as flowering currant and forsythia.

MAKING MORE PLANTS

They root readily from cuttings. Hardwood cuttings are the least trouble, especially as you can leave them outside in a nursery trench all winter. Softwood or semi-ripe cuttings need to be grown in a cold frame for best results.

CARING FOR PLANTS

Prune branches back after they have flowered. When bushes get older, take out a few gnarled stems right back to the ground to rejuvenate the plant. Mulch with well-rotted manure.

The 'Florida Variegata' hybrid of weigela has wrinkled leaves edged in creamy white.

Index

index

143